BATHROOM of NORTHERN CALIFORNIA TRIVIA

Weird, Wacky and Wild

Monica Woelfel & Lisa Wojna
Illustrations by Patrick Hénaff,
Roger Garcia & Graham Johnson

BLUE
BIKE
BOOKS

© 2007 by Blue Bike Books
First printed in 2007 10 9 8 7 6 5 4 3 2 1
Printed in Canada

The Publisher: Blue Bike Books
www.bluebikebooks.com

Library and Archives Canada Cataloguing in Publication

Woelfel, Monica, 1966–
   Bathroom book of Northern California trivia : weird, wacky and wild /
Monica Woelfel and Lisa Wojna.

ISBN-13: 978-1-897278-23-9
ISBN-10: 1-897278-23-3

   1. California, Northern—Miscellanea. I. Wojna, Lisa, 1962– II. Title.

F867.5.W64 2007   979.4   C2007-901521-2

Project Director: Nicholle Carrière
Project Editor: Tom Monto
Cover Image: Roger Garcia
Illustrations: Patrick Hénaff, Roger Garcia, Graham Johnson

We acknowledge the support of the Alberta Foundation for the Arts for our publishing program.

PC: 5

DEDICATION

To my nieces and nephews, who are anything but "trivial" in my life: Aidan, Henry, George, Noah, Quinn, Shayla and Sofia.

—Monica

ACKNOWLEDGMENTS

Thanks to Nicholle at Blue Bike Books for giving me the chance to work on this fun and fascinating project and for bringing the entire series to life. Thanks to Tom Monto for his keen eye for detail and skillful edits. Thanks to all of my friends who sent me their favorite eccentric bits of knowledge about this weird and wonderful place we call northern California. (Jordan, Carla and Randy, I think you get the prize for the most eccentric bits of all.) Thanks to my family, especially Rebecca, Dave, Sofia and Quinn, who were patient with me while I holed up for hours doing research. And, finally, a big thanks to Mike who put up with this phrase on a daily (hourly?) basis, "Hey, did you know...?"

—Monica

Many thanks to: my clever editor Tom, who pieced together the work of two authors and did so seamlessly; to my mentor Faye, who always gives more of herself than required; and to my family—my husband Garry, sons Peter, Matthew, Nathan, daughter Melissa and granddaughter Jada. Without you, all this and anything else I do in my life would be meaningless.

—Lisa

CONTENTS

INTRODUCTION

When I first started this book, I had just moved back to Northern California after many years living out of state. I didn't know if I would stay. I was impatient with Californians, the way I'm sometimes impatient with my own family members. I thought, *People in northern California are so...* fill in the blank: relaxed, politically correct, overly friendly, outdoorsy (I mean, does *everyone* jog?).

Rounding up trivia for this book showed me that Northern California is more diverse than most people would ever guess, with its dairymen/women (the state's number one agricultural product is dairy) and bus drivers, its biotech research scientists (groundbreaking Genentech started in San Francisco) and retail clerks, its realtors, farm workers, engineers and teachers. There are duck hunters as well as birdwatchers, NASCAR fans at Sonoma's Infineon Raceway (formerly Sears Point), as well as big-wall rock climbers in Yosemite.

And then there are all those people for whom Northern California is famous: San Francisco drag queens, elite surfers who say "dude" a lot, woodsy park rangers who always dress in green (even when out of uniform), the Breasts-Not-Bombs Berkeley political activists (I'm not sure what boobs have to do with world peace, but I'm sure one of them could tell you) and the "agricultural producers" in the remote hills of Humboldt County.

As you read this book, every now and then you'll come across a little Northern versus Southern California rivalry. The two sister regions are very different (that's why we've got a book of trivia for each). All the people down there really do seem to be bronzed, buff surfers. They talk "valley," and their freeways make a Northern Californian's head spin. But, as with most siblings, we regard one other with friendly amusement. In the end, we're all Californians.

The great thing about trivia (I've learned) is that it doesn't deal just with "important" information, such as major wars and gross domestic products. It also tells about the everyday moments (weirdnesses, if you will) of real people's lives. I loved learning, for instance, that some of Northern California's Native Americans considered a woodpecker scalp a sign of wealth (and why not?!), or that the only reason Sir Francis Drake bothered to step ashore here at all was that his ship's holds were bursting with booty stolen from the Spanish. Learning other information, such as the facts that there were anti-Chinese riots in 1870s San Francisco and that that city segregated Japanese-American schoolchildren in 1905, made me sad, but also taught me about my home.

Surprisingly, writing this book has completed my homecoming. I had moved back ambivalent, as I said, to the place where my mother and her mother were born—and, as the trivia-gathering process came to an end, I realized that I had gotten to know my home region—warts and all. The result is that I've grown hugely fond of this place with all its quirks. I'm proud of the hardworking residents of our Central Valley who grow and harvest the food much of the nation puts on its table. I'm delighted that Northern Californians invented Frisbees and boysenberries. I'm awed that some of our beautiful redwood trees have been around since the year zero (as in 0000). What a place!

I hope that, whether you're a visitor or a resident, this collection of trivia will do for you what it has done for me—paint a portrait of Northern California that's quirkier and more entertaining than any history book or travel guide could do. Most of all, I guess, I hope it makes you think and makes you laugh. Because, as Northern Californians can tell you, "laid back" really does live longer.

WHAT SETS NORTHERN CALIFORNIA APART

Amazing Trees

Northern California is home to some of the most amazing (and record-breaking) trees on the planet.

A Massive Tree

A tree called the General Sherman sequoia (a.k.a. redwood or giant sequoia) in Sequoia National Park is the world's most massive living inhabitant. With a trunk 103 feet around and standing nearly 275 feet tall, old Sherman is made up of an estimated 52,508 cubic feet of wood. That's a whole lot of tree. It is estimated to be between 1800 and 2700 years old.

You Think *That's* Old?!

Amazing as a 2000-year-old tree is, the oldest living thing on Earth is a bristlecone pine in northern California's White Mountains just north of Death Valley. Nicknamed "Methusaleh" (as in "older than…"), after the

969-year-old geezer in the Bible, the tree is estimated to be 4650 years old.

In other words, it was a sprout in the Bronze Age, when the Chinese had just figured out how to make bronze and people in Mesopotamia were first starting to write—on cuneiform tablets.

Tallest Tree in the World

"Hyperion" is the name given to the tallest tree known on Earth, measuring 379 feet tall—about the height of a 40-story building. Hyperion is a coast redwood (*Sequoia sempervirens*), a close cousin of the giant sequoia (*Sequoiadendron giganteum*), the same species as the famous General Sherman. Hyperion grows in an undisclosed, remote location in Redwood National Park near Eureka.

Big GSP

California's gross state product was $1.622 trillion in 2006, according to the U.S. Department of Commerce. That makes the state's economy the eighth largest of any *country* in the world.

Gnarliest Wave

Elite surfers compete at a spot called "Mavericks" just outside Half Moon Bay, where some of the world's biggest monster waves (some cresting as high as 100 feet) break over a boulder reef.

Hearst Castle

The famed estate of newspaperman William Randolph Hearst—the Mediterranean Revival–style Hearst Castle in San Simeon—has a combined indoor area (in its various "casas") of over 90,000 square feet, complete with 165 rooms, 14 sitting rooms, 38 bedrooms, 61 bathrooms, two libraries, a billiard room, a movie theater, a dining hall, 41 fireplaces and 127 acres of landscaped gardens. These days, the Hearst family is no longer in residence, and visitors are invited to tour the sumptuous grounds.

Tons of Fruits and Nuts

The top five counties for agricultural sales are all in Northern and Central California—Fresno, Tulare, Monterey, Kern and Merced. Together they produce over 40 percent of the state's total crop income.

California produces 100 percent of the nation's almonds! That's 915 million pounds of the tasty nuts (not counting shells) in 2005. Meanwhile, the state produced six million tons of grapes the same year, accounting for over 90 percent of grapes grown in the U.S. and bringing in more than $3 billion.

Eagles

The largest winter population of bald eagles—over 1000 birds— in the lower 48 states calls the Klamath Basin National Wildlife Refuge, on the northern California–Oregon border, home. (Or they would, if they could speak English.)

DID YOU KNOW?

Experts estimate that 200 languages are spoken in California.

World Peace Central
The United Nations was founded in San Francisco in April 1945.

Growing Fast

From 1960 to 2000, California grew at twice the national average rate. This means that every year, the state added 500,000 new people, a group the size of everyone in the city of Long Beach.

The number of Hispanic citizens in the state is increasing every year. In fact, today one in three Californians is of Hispanic origin. *Andale!*

The "Say Hey" Kid
Hall of Famer Willie Mays played for the San Francisco Giants for 14 years.

Diego Rivera

There are four of the renowned Mexican painter Diego Rivera's murals in Northern California.

UC Berkeley

Northern California is home to UC Berkeley (founded in 1868), the first university of the state's prestigious post-secondary education system.

Fore!

Golf Digest magazine has consistently named Pebble Beach Resort in Monterey as one of the world's top golf destinations.

Mount Shasta

Way up north, Mount Shasta, at 14,162 feet tall, is the tallest volcano in California and the second tallest in the U.S.

IN THE BEGINNING

What's in a Name?

If the meaning behind a name bears any responsibility for the personality of a place, it's no wonder California is a mysterious land where almost anything goes and imagination rules. *Las Sergas de Esplandia* was a wild romance written by Gracia Montalvo in 1510. The story told of an island named California, which abounded in pearls and gold. Inhabited solely by a race of Amazonian black women, men were welcomed to its shores only once a year and only for one purpose—to procreate. Any man attempting access to its shores at any other time was killed and fed to the griffins.

In any case, early explorers searching for pearls thought they'd discovered the mythical land of Montalvo's story. And despite the somewhat tumultuous development of the state, during which many nations attempted to lay claim to the land, the name stuck.

DID YOU  KNOW?

The ownership of California was obviously a contentious issue. At different points in its early history, Russia, Spain, Mexico and the United States all erected flags on California soil, each laying claim to the state.

Also Known As

California's nickname is the Golden State. The moniker was made official in 1968. Although some think it refers to the Gold Rush of California's early history, it actually refers to the California hillsides, which typically turn a golden brown during the summer months.

Making It Official

California received its admission to statehood on September 9, 1850, making it the 31st state of the union.

SYMBOLS AND EMBLEMS

State Motto

Literally translated, California's state motto *Eureka* means, "I have found it." It is thought the term initially referred to the discovery of gold in California. The motto was officially adopted in 1963, despite earlier attempts to adopt the more traditional "In God We Trust."

Flying High

The original state flag was first raised on June 14, 1846—four years before California received state status. William Todd painted this first version as a visible statement that the American settlers of the Sonoma area weren't happy with the Mexican government that ruled California at the time. In what became known as the "Bear Flag Revolt," the Americans erected the flag, consisting of a grizzly bear, a five-pointed, red star and the words "California Republic" painted on little more than a scrap of brown cotton.

A modern version of this original flag was officially adopted in 1911. Sadly, the original flag was destroyed in the "Great Earthquake and Fire of 1906."

Official State Animal

Given its prominence on the state flag, it's no surprise that California's state animal is the California grizzly bear (*Ursus californicus*). It sadly earned this honor in 1953, a full 31 years after the last of this "largest and most powerful of carnivores" roaming the lowlands of the state was killed.

DID YOU KNOW?

The last California Grizzly was hunted down and killed in Tulare County in August 1922.

Assorted State Symbols

☛ The Great Seal—a picturesque snapshot of California with the Roman goddess Minerva featured prominently along with 31 stars representing the states of the union—was officially adopted during the Constitutional Convention of 1849. Of course, California didn't officially become a state until the next year, but that seemed nothing more than a minor inconvenience.

☛ The golden poppy (*Eschsholtzia californica*), which grows wild throughout the state, was named California's official flower in 1903. It's so popular, that in 1974, the legislature designated April 6 as "California Poppy Day."

☛ The California Valley quail (*Lophortyx californica*) was adopted as the state bird in 1931.

☛ Among California's first official symbols was the Pasadena Playhouse. It was honored by being named the official state theater in 1937.

☛ California's native redwood was named the state's official tree in 1937, but this initial designation didn't mention a specific species of redwood. Since California has two species of redwood that are considered native to the state—the coast redwood (*Sequoia sempervirens*) and the giant sequoia (*Sequoiadendron giganteum*)—both were given the distinction with an amended declaration in 1953.

☛ Blue and gold were adopted as the official state colors in 1951. The color blue represents the sky, and gold represents the color of the precious metal that initiated a flood of miners to the area in the early days of the state's history.

☛ The California golden trout (*Salmo augua-bonita*) was named the state's official fish in 1947.

☛ "I Love You, California," penned by F.B. Silverwood, put to music by A.F. Frankenstein and first published in 1913, was named the state's official song in 1951.

☛ Since gold fever resulted, in part anyway, in the population explosion California experienced in the years following the metal's discovery in the state in 1848, it makes sense that gold is the state's official mineral. It was so named in 1965.

☛ Serpentine was named California's official rock in 1965.

☛ Unique to the foothills of the Sierra Nevada and costal areas from Sonoma to San Diego, the California dogface butterfly (*Zerene eurydice*) was named the state's official insect in 1972.

☛ The desert tortoise is not only protected by the dubious honor of "endangered species" status, it was also named California's official state reptile in 1972.

☛ The California gray whale (*Eschrichtius robustus*), which measures up to 50 feet in length and weighs in anywhere between 20 and 40 tons, was named California's official marine mammal in 1975.

☛ In 1979, the state legislature designated the California Historical Society its official historical society.

☛ The blue diamond—as rare and precious as it is expensive—was named California's state gemstone in 1985. The blue beauty, also known as benitoite, was first discovered in California in the San Benito River.

☛ The long-toothed, ferocious meat-eater known as *Smilodon californicus* (the sabre-toothed cat) was named the state's official fossil in 1973. The feline, which lived about 11,000 years ago, earned this honor because abundant skeletal remains of the cat have been discovered in the tar pits of Rancho La Brea in Los Angeles.

☛ Although its roots can be traced back to the swing, whip or jitterbug dances of the 1930s, West Coast swing is a 100-percent-pure California product. It's no wonder, then, that it was named the state's official dance in 1988. The state's official folk dance—none other than the square dance—was also declared that same year.

☛ California was the first state to designate an official prehistoric artifact. What appears to be a miniature bear carved from volcanic rock was uncovered during a dig in San Diego County in 1985. Measuring 2.5 by 1.5 inches, the Chipped Stone Bear was named the state's official prehistoric artifact in 1991.

- Patriotic to the core, California adopted the California Consolidated Drum Band as its official fife-and-drum band in 1997.

- San Joaquin soil was named California's official state soil in 1997, but really, who knew soil could be so interesting? According to some sources, San Joaquin soil could be up to 250,000 years old and was one of the original soils studied in the state. The 1997 designation coincided with "the completion of the state's most comprehensive soil inventory," thereby acknowledging the "importance of soil."

- Being a gold rush state, it's no wonder California has a designated, official gold rush ghost town. The town of Bodie earned the title in 2002. During its boom, the town of Bodie had a population of about 10,000. Located northeast of Yosemite and south of Bridgeport, the town stands as a visual reminder of a bygone era and was named a National Historic Site and a California State Historic Park in 1962.

- California has an official state military museum, and it is none other than the California State Military Museum and Resource Center, located in the Old Sacramento State Historic Park. It received its official designation in 2004.

- Purple needlegrass (*Nassella pulchra*) was named California's official grass in 2004.

- The blue, green, red and gold of the John Muir family tartan was the basis for California's official tartan. Officially adopted in 2001, the tartan was chosen in honor of the state's well-loved "naturalist, explorer and conservationist." Incidentally, a year later the state legislature also declared April 6 as "California Tartan Day."

AVERAGES AND EXTREMES

A Land of Extremes

When it comes to weather and climate, many consider California a land of extremes. It's a land where, depending on proximity to the Pacific Ocean, mountain ranges and area elevation, climate can vary from subtropical to subarctic. Death Valley is one of the hottest, driest locations on Earth, while northern portions of the state receive considerably higher levels of precipitation than their southern counterparts. The Sierra Nevadas are higher in elevation and therefore see a greater snowfall than other parts of the state. They also see milder summers than those seen in the desert.

Temperature Comparisons

San Francisco
- Average annual temperature is 58.6°
- Average summer high temperature is 70°
- Average winter high temperature is 60°
- Average summer low is 52°
- Average winter low temperature is 47°
- Highest temperature on record is 87° in 2006
- Lowest temperature on record is 36° in 1856

Sacramento
- Average annual temperature is 61°
- Average summer high temperature is 93°
- Average winter high temperature is 46°
- Average summer low is 60.2°
- Average winter low temperature is 41.2°
- Highest temperature on record is 115° in 2006
- Lowest temperature on record is 17° in 1932

Annual Rainfall

Average annual rainfall varies considerably in California, with Inyo County recording a mere two inches each year and Del Norte County recording as much as 80 inches.

Wide Range in Precipitation

- ☞ You can expect at least 50 inches of precipitation in areas surrounding the northwest portion of the Sierra Nevadas.
- ☞ San Francisco and Monterey Bay areas might only see 20 inches in a year.
- ☞ Death Valley can expect less than two inches of annual rainfall.

Thunderstorms

- ☞ Thunderstorms can occur year-round throughout California.
- ☞ Areas of higher elevation, such as the Sierra Nevadas, see thunderstorms of varying severity about 55 days each year.

Let it Snow

- ☞ Almost every part of California has experienced snowfall, though snow is most common in mountain areas.
- ☞ DeathValley may be an arid desert, but snow does fall there. Although it is more common in the desert's higher elevations, snow has also been recorded in low-lying areas.

DID YOU KNOW?

Snow is rare in Sacramento—but not entirely unheard of. Usually the city receives a dusting of snow every decade or so. But on January 4, 1888, the city recorded its largest-ever snowfall, at 3.5 inches. It's a record that stands to this day.

Average Growing Season

The southernmost portion of Northern California boasts a growing season between 250 and 325 days long. The average growing season in the Sierra Nevada region, on the other hand, is 50 days.

THE WORST WEATHER

Tornadoes

California, on average, only experiences about six tornadoes a year, based on statistics gathered between 1951 and 2000. Most occur in or south of the Central Valley.

Walls of Water

Surfs crest along the California coastline throughout the year, but in the spring, they measure about five feet or so—a perfect crest for an avid surfer. However, since the average water temperature along the San Francisco coastline is around 50°, folks tend to prefer California's more southern beaches. Water temperatures there average about 10° warmer.

DID YOU KNOW?

Death Valley earns top spot as the hottest place on earth. From July 6 to August 17, 1917, the area recorded 43 consecutive days of temperatures higher than 120°.

DID YOU  KNOW?

Since 1852, San Francisco has only had six documented instances of an inch or more of snowfall in a single day. The last time the city experienced such a snowfall was in 1932. Its highest recorded snowfall was on February 5, 1887, when the downtown weather bureau measured 3.7 inches.

Droughts
California routinely experiences extended periods of drought, some as long as 80 years in duration. One source points to the year 1625 as California's driest in history but says the state generally had considerable rainfall during the last part of the 1900s.

Weather Extremes
- Highest recorded temperature: 134°, DeathValley, July 10, 1913
- Lowest recorded temperature: −45°, Boca, January 20, 1937
- Largest amount of rainfall in one hour: 4.7 inches, Mt. Palomar, August 13, 1992
- Largest amount of rainfall in 24 hours: 26 inches, Hoegees Camp, January 22, 1943
- Largest amount of rainfall in one month: 82 inches, Camp 6, December 1981
- Largest amount of seasonal rainfall: 257 inches, Camp 6, 1982
- Smallest amount of seasonal rainfall: 0.00 inches, DeathValley, 1929
- Largest amount of snowfall in 24 hours: 67 inches, Echo Summit, January 4–5, 1982
- Largest amount of storm snowfall—189 inches, Shasta Ski Bowl, February 13–19, 1959.
- Largest amount of snowfall in one month: 390 inches, Tamarack, January 1911
- Largest amount of snowfall in one season: 884 inches, Tamarack, 1906–07
- Deepest ground snow cover: 451 inches, Tamarack, March 11, 1911
- Highest wind velocity: 101 mph, Sandberg, March 25, 1975

California's Worst Weather Disasters of the Last 100 Years (according to the National Weather Services Forecast Office)

15. Storms at Sea
In 1939, the California coast was hit with a tropical storm of near hurricane proportions. Along with torrential rains dumping almost six inches of precipitation in just 24 hours, 45 deaths were reported on land alone.

14. Fire and Complications
On September 3, 2004, a wildfire flashed to life near Geysers, the world's largest geothermal power plant, located 72 miles north of San Francisco in the Mayacamas Mountains. Hot, dry weather and high winds fanned the flames and the fire grew rapidly, threatening homes and vineyards in the Alexander Valley and Pine Flat areas. By September 5, the fire was estimated to cover 6000 acres. It burned 14,000 acres before it was quenched, but fortunately, no lives were lost.

13. Storms-a-Plenty
A winter full of excessive rain and windstorms resulted in 28 deaths and $1.8 billion in damage in 1995, ranking it the state's 13th-worst weather-related disaster of the 1900s.

12. Christmas Disaster
It was a watery Christmas in central and northern California back in 1955. Floods that year caused rivers to overflow, resulting in 74 deaths and $200 million in damages.

11. Deep Freeze
For folks in the Midwest, 25° may not seem all that frigid. But, in California in December 1990, three to five days of

temperatures lower than 26° represented all-time lows, and 33 counties were declared disaster areas. An estimated $3.4 billion in damage resulted. Much of that was damage to the state's agricultural economy.

10. Heavy Precipitation
Snow and rain combined to create disastrous effects in the winter of 1969. With 47 dead, 161 injured and $300 million in losses, 40 counties were declared disaster areas.

9. Dust in the Wind
Winds gusting 192 miles per hour in Arvin in December 1977 quite literally changed the landscape. More than 25 million tons of soil literally drifted away, and once fertile farmland was transformed into sandy soil. Along with three deaths and $40 million in immediate economic losses, the agriculture industry in the area suffered for many years after the storm.

8. Water, Water, Everywhere
Flooding in March 1907 and January 1909 forced state officials to rethink flood control designs. These floods caused flooding on all major rivers in the Sacramento Valley. In 1907 alone, more than 300,000 acres were waterlogged.

7. Great Balls of Fire
In October 1993, dry winds propelled 20 separate fires gone awry across southern California. The resulting carnage included four dead, 162 injured, 194,000 acres of property damaged and $1 billion in economic losses.

6. Flooding Complications
A March 1964 earthquake in Alaska turned into a California disaster when a resulting tsunami hit coastal areas in and around Del Norte County. The tidal wave struck Crescent City, destroying 150 buildings and killing 11 people.

5. Flooding out the New Year

From December 26, 1996, to January 3, 1997, rain fell throughout north and central California almost steadily. The Yosemite Valley—an area that hadn't experienced flooding since 1861–62—was located in the 300-square-mile area that flooded. Eight people were killed and 2000 businesses were damaged or destroyed along with 23,000 homes.

4. Firestorm

Hot, dry weather and strong winds strengthened a fire that broke out in the Oakland Hills in October 1991. The fire caused 25 dead, 150 injured, and almost $2 billion in damage to homes and apartments in just a 24-hour period.

3. Colder Still

Orange and other citrus fruit crops suffered, in some cases, irreparable damage when temperatures dipped below 15° for several days in January 1913. While the exact amount of damage isn't available, the extreme weather led to the development of the fruit frost forecast program.

2. Drought

There's no doubt that, moderation is the key when it comes to precipitation. While excessive moisture has caused no end of problems throughout history, drought has been just as damaging. Drought conditions in California, extending from 1975 to 1977, resulted in disaster declarations in 31 counties and $2.6 billion in economic losses.

1. El Niño

Excessive precipitation, damaging winds, mudslides and overflowing rivers across most of the state—all were the result of El Niño storms in 1982 and 1983. Forty-six of California's 58 counties were declared disaster areas. About 36 people were killed and 481 injured, with almost 8000 homes and businesses damaged or destroyed.

GENERAL GEOGRAPHY

The Big Picture

Generally speaking, the geography of Northern California can be divided into six main regions: the Klamath Mountains; Coastal Ranges; the Sierra Nevadas; Central Valley; Cascade Mountains; and the Basin and Range Region.

Location, Location, Location

The 770-mile-long and 250-mile-wide state of California is located on the country's Pacific coast, bordered by Oregon to the north, Nevada and Arizona to the east and Mexico to the south.

Overall Size

California is the third largest U.S. state. Covering an area of 163,707 square miles, it seriously lags behind Texas, which is in second place with 268,601 square miles, and behind first-place Alaska with its 656,424 square miles.

Surf and Turf

Of its area, 155,973 square miles are land, and 7734 square miles are water. Forests cover about 35 percent of California's landmass, while deserts take up about 25 percent.

Sandy Beaches

While the state only measures 770 miles long, the California coastline extends for about 840 miles. This is roughly three-quarters of the contiguous U.S. Pacific coastline.

Highest Point

Mount Shasta is the tallest peak in northern California, standing at 14,162 feet.

Lowest Point

Punching in at 282 feet below sea level, California's Death Valley is indeed a deadly place to all but the hardiest. It is also widely considered the lowest place in the Western Hemisphere and one of the hottest places on earth.

Desert Parkland

Death Valley—an apt name for a corner of the California desert so desolate and barren only the most hardy can survive. Essentially the valley floor beneath Telescope Peak, Death Valley covers about 3000 square miles. Average yearly precipitation in this arid climate is less than two inches, and temperatures can soar as high as 134°—the all-time record set in 1913.

DID YOU  KNOW?

The only place in the world that's claimed a higher daily temperature than Death Valley is Libya. In 1936, Libya registered a suffocating 136°.

Center Point
The geographic center of California is 38 miles east of the city of Madera.

Major Rivers
Two of California's most important rivers are the Sacramento and the San Joaquin. The 382-mile-long Sacramento River, which is considered the state's longest river, flows through the northern portion of California's Central Valley. The San Joaquin is California's second longest river, at 330 miles. Its waters are used to irrigate farmland east of the Central Valley.

Capital City
The city of Sacramento, which was founded in 1849 and is the oldest incorporated city in California, is the state capital. Population-wise, Sacramento, with roughly 407,000 residents, is the seventh largest city in the state.

COUNTIES GALORE

While there is no official designation for where Northern California starts, many people agree that the culture shifts just north of the city of Santa Barbara. That puts the following counties in northern California: Alameda, Alpine, Amador, Butte, Calaveras, Colusa, Contra Costa, Del Norte, El Dorado, Fresno, Glenn, Humboldt, Inyo, (parts of) Kern, Kings, Lake, Lassen, Madera, Marin, Mariposa, Mendocino, Merced, Modoc, Mono, Monterey, Napa, Nevada, Placer, Plumas, Sacramento, San Benito, San Francisco, San Joaquin, San Luis Obispo, San Mateo, Santa Clara, Santa Cruz, Shasta, Sierra, Siskiyou, Solano, Sonoma, Stanislaus, Sutter, Tehama, Trinity, Tulare, Tuolumne, Yolo and Yuba.

County Curiosities

☞ Alameda was formed from portions of two existing counties, Contra Costa and Santa Clara, on March 25, 1853.

☞ Alpine County, with a population of 1159 people, based on 2005 census estimates, is the state's least populated county.

☞ Amador, named after Jose Maria Amador, is the only county in the state named after a native Californian.

☞ Butte County's motto is "Land of Natural Wealth and Beauty." Founded on February 18, 1850, Butte was one of California's founding counties.

☞ Built in 1861 and given the designation of California State Historic Landmark in 1976, the original Colusa County Courthouse is still open for business.

☞ Contra Costa County was one of California's original counties and is currently ranked the state's ninth most populated.

- Calaveras County's claim to fame is the fact renowned author Mark Twain set his short story "The Celebrated Jumping Frog of Calaveras County" there.

- Tucked away in the northwest corner of northern California is Del Norte. The county is well known for its amazing redwoods.

- There are 20 pioneer cemeteries listed on the El Dorado County website.

- Fresno is considered the nation's number one agricultural county.

- Glenn County is another of northern California's agricultural leaders, with about 1188 working farms.

- Including county, state and federal designations, Humboldt boasts close to 30 percent of its land as parkland.

- Kern County is California's third largest county and is commonly referred to as "California's Golden Empire."

☞ The "Landmark Tree" of Kings County was considered a guiding light, of sorts, to travelers to the area back in the 1800s. The large sycamore still stands, located on Lacey Boulevard.

☞ Along with its many lakes, Lake County is well known for its lush wine grapes, pears and other farm produce.

☞ Lassen County is home to Lassen Peak and Lassen Volcanic National Park. Lassen Peak last erupted on May 22, 1915.

☞ Madera is the geographic center of California.

☞ Frank Lloyd Wright, one of the country's most prolific architects, designed the Marin County Civic Center. The building is considered a State Designated Historic Landmark.

☞ Mariposa County is lovingly nicknamed the "Mother of Counties." This is because it gave birth, if you will, to 11 other counties. These counties were annexed from Mariposa's original area.

☞ In the spring of 2004, Mendocino County became the first county in the nation to ban GM (genetically modified) crops.

☞ Merced County is home to Yosemite National Park.

☞ Modoc County's only incorporated city is Alturas, with a population of 9449.

☞ Ninety-four percent of the 3030 square miles of Mono County is publicly owned land.

☞ Parts of Monterey County, which was originally incorporated in 1850, were annexed to help form San Benito County in 1874.

☞ There is more to Napa County than the wines of the Napa Valley, but the wine certainly brings in the tourists.

- One of Nevada County's obscure hidden treasures is the lone grave of a toddler buried along the Emigrant Trail back in 1858.

- You can still pan for gold in the American, Yuba and Bear Rivers of Placer County.

- There are more than 100 lakes, 1000 rivers and one million acres of forest in Plumas County.

- There are more than 20 museums in Sacramento County.

- San Benito County was formed in 1874 from parts of Monterey and other counties.

- San Francisco County is home to China Beach, Fisherman's Wharf, Alcatraz (a prison turned state park) and, of course, the Golden Gate Bridge.

- San Joaquin County takes its name from the San Joaquin River, California's second largest river.

- Father Junipero Serra founded the Mission San Luis Obispo de Tolosa, located in San Luis Obispo County, in 1772. The mission, which is located in downtown San Luis Obispo, still operates as a church.

- The county name of San Mateo is Spanish for Saint Matthew.

- Santa Clara County is the heart of Silicon Valley, which earned this moniker after journalist Don Hoefler wrote a series on the area entitled "Silicon Valley USA" in the publication *Electronic News*. The term silicon was in direct reference to the high number of computer-related industries in the area.

- With 300-plus days of sunshine and relatively low humidity, the climate of Santa Cruz County is said to be Mediterranean in character.

☛ Shasta County is home to Weaverville Joss House. Built in 1874, it's said to be the oldest, continuously used Chinese temple in California.

☛ The entire population of Sierra County is 3555, according to 2000 census figures. With an area of 963 square miles, that means folks in that county each have more than one-quarter of a square mile of space to call their own.

☛ Siskiyou County is considered one of the most ecologically diverse areas of the world.

☛ Inyo County calls itself the adventure capital of the world. This is likely because both California's highest point, Mount Whitney, and its lowest elevation, Death Valley, as well as everything in between are found there.

☛ There are 116 county-owned bridges in Solano County.

☛ A great pastime on the coast of Sonoma County during December and January is whale watching.

☛ Agriculture is the major industry in Stanislaus County.

☛ Native Americans of the Maidu tribe originally inhabited Sutter County.

- Tehama County (also called Tehama Country) is proud of its natural beauty. So much so, in fact, that its motto is "Tehama County…where Mother Nature and Father Time are still an item."

- Although Weaverville is the county seat of Trinity County, it is not an incorporated city. In fact, though it has a population of 13,022 and is far from the least populated of northern California's counties, Trinity County doesn't have a single incorporated city.

- Most of the eastern portion of Tulare County is public land. This includes Sequoia National Park and National Forest and the Mineral King, Golden Trout, and Domelands Wilderness areas.

- Tuolumne County, pronounced "To all o' me," is a Native American name with several possible meanings, including "Many Stone Houses," the "Land of Mountain Lions" and "Straight Up Steep."

- Yolo County produces about 90 percent of the tomatoes grown in the entire country.

- Explorer Captain John Sutter named Yuba County after the Yuba River.

DID YOU KNOW?

The entire Mariposa County doesn't have a single operational traffic light. It's considered California's largest county to be able to make such a claim.

EARTHQUAKE CENTRAL

The possibility of an earthquake is one of the scary features of life in California.

- ☛ The first major earthquake of record in California occurred in 1769 in the Los Angeles region.
- ☛ Shockwaves were felt along the San Andreas Fault from Fort Tejon to Los Angeles, San Francisco and Sacramento in January 1857.
- ☛ InOctober 1868, 30 people were killed after an earthquake in central California shook the Hayward Fault, a main branch of the San Andreas Fault. This earthquake was the first to earn the name the "Great Earthquake."

- ☛ In March 1876, an earthquake along the Sierra Nevada Fault system killed 27 people and destroyed more than 100 homes.
- ☛ On April 19, 1892, an earthquake damaged or destroyed brick and frame buildings alike in Vacaville.
- ☛ One of the greatest earthquakes ever to hit California, the earthquake of April 18, 1906, killed 700. Resulting fires raged throughout San Francisco, and the end cost was estimated at more than $500 million.
- ☛ The November 1927 earthquake near Lompoc caused damage to hillsides.
- ☛ TheKern County earthquake of July 1952 took 12 lives and caused countless injuries and $60 million in property damage.
- ☛ The 1989 "Loma Prieta" quake in the San Francisco Bay area collapsed the Nimitz Freeway, killing 42 drivers.

Table Manners and Plate Tectonics

You know how sometimes when you eat, say, a cookie, how little crumbs stick to the corners of your lips? So embarrassing. Well, the last time the North American and Pacific tectonic plates collided in California, one of them left crumbs along the "lips" of the other. Am I losing you? Here, I'll explain.

The Point Reyes Peninsula, in western Marin County, is completely different geologically from the land just inland of it. Scientists say that's because the Peninsula broke off from the Pacific Plate, while the rest of the state is part of the North American Plate. The line running between the two is the San Andreas fault, ground zero for northern California's famous earthquakes. In the 1906 quake, Point Reyes moved five yards north along the Marin coastline. Weird, huh?

DID YOU KNOW?

California records about 500,000 seismic tremors each year.

Spacy Landscape

If you think the Trona Pinnacles look like something out of
a Star Trek movie, you may not be as off base as you think.
These geological wonders are used as a backdrop for as many as
30 film projects annually. Of those, more than a dozen have
become well-known movie hits, including *The Gate II, Lost in
Space, Planet of the Apes* and, of course, *Star Trek V*.

DID YOU KNOW?

You might scratch your head in wonder at this little tidbit, but
in 2003, a Whiskeytown National Recreation Area park ranger
named Russ Weatherbee tracked down a 300-foot waterfall that
seemed to have disappeared, if you use the park's circa-1960s
map as a guideline. Apparently, the waterfall wasn't anywhere
near the location marked on the map, but after much determi-
nation and a lot of hard work, Russ tracked it down near
Crystal Creek.

VEGETATION

Towering Overhead

As if dictated by its diverse geography, California is considered by some to be the most ecologically diverse state in the United States.

It may be younger than once thought, but one of the world's most majestic and largest redwoods still calls Sequoia National Park home. General Sherman, a giant sequoia, was so named by soldiers in the American Civil War in 1879.

Standing 275 feet tall and measuring 30 feet in diameter at its base, General Sherman was thought to be close to 6000 years old, but today folks at the Western Ecological Research Center estimate its age at closer to 2000 years.

The tallest redwood known to date is called Hyperion. It's a coast redwood (as opposed to the giant sequoia species of General Sherman) located in an undisclosed, remote region of Humboldt County. Hyperion stands a dizzying 379.1 feet tall.

Beauty in Blue

It's as blue as the California sky and has as beautiful a bloom as you've ever seen. The California lilac (*Ceanothus*) grows well throughout most of the state. The shrub, which can grow taller than five feet, usually blooms in May and June. Considered an evergreen, it remains green year-round unless temperatures dip lower than 15°.

DID YOU KNOW?

About 30 percent of the roughly 5000 species of plant life growing in California are endemic to the state, growing nowhere else in the world. Most of these rare beauties grow in California because of its unique geological history and climactic conditions.

Odd and Obscure

The sand-loving phlox (*Phlox cuspidata*) might live smack dab in the middle of the Mojave Desert, but it's only visible in years where rainfall is higher than average. The ground-hugging cover grows quite sparsely, not in obvious bunches, and you actually have to look for it to find it. When there aren't prime growing conditions, the perennial plant seems to go into hibernation, waiting for just the right time to burst forth in purplish blossoms.

About 35 percent of the state of California is covered in forests. The densest are in the area of the Klamath Mountains and the Coast Ranges north of San Francisco and near the Sierra Nevadas.

Disappearing Giants

While the state is well known for its redwoods, California forests are constantly under attack by urban sprawl. Between 1992 and 1997, 244,000 acres disappeared, adding to the more than 80 percent of coast redwoods and the 70 percent of ancient forests in the Sierra Nevada that have already been lost.

ENVIRONMENTAL ALTERCATIONS

The Slickens

During the 1800s, hydraulic gold mines in Northern California swept aside entire hillsides with high-powered hoses. Meanwhile, the "slickens," as people called the goo that washed downriver, killed farmers' orchards, swamped boats and even engulfed houses. The 1884 court case *Woodruff v. North Bloomfield Gravel Mining Company* (but widely called the "Sawyer decision") ordered a clean-up of the hydraulic miners' pollution. The Sawyer decision is hailed as the first environmental lawsuit in the state.

The Sierra Club

John Muir, who once described himself as a "poetico-trampo-geologist-botanist and ornithologist-naturalist," founded the Sierra Club in 1892 to protect the natural world. Until his death in 1914, Muir served as president of the club, which helped establish the nation's national park system and has been at the forefront of environmental preservation ever since.

Yosemite

Naturalist John Muir helped convince the U.S. Congress to name 1500 square miles around the spectacular Yosemite Valley as California's first national park in 1890. Concerned that the valley itself needed greater protection, Muir talked President Theodore Roosevelt into visiting Yosemite in 1903. As a result, the entire Yosemite Valley was included in Yosemite National Park in 1906.

Sacred Places

Environmentalist David Brower invoked one of the most beautiful and sacred places in civilization—the Sistine Chapel—in his (alas, futile) struggle to prevent the construction of a dam that would flood a place he found both beautiful and sacred, Glen Canyon. His ad campaign asked, "Should we also flood the Sistine Chapel so tourists can get nearer the ceiling?"

DID YOU  KNOW?

President Abraham Lincoln first extended protection to the stunning Yosemite area. In 1864, Lincoln deeded areas around the valley and the nearby Mariposa Grove to the State of California as its first public preserve. This was the first time in history that the federal government had set aside lands in order to protect them for public enjoyment.

Protecting the Giants

On December 10, 1997, a 23-year-old woman scaled one of northern California's towering coast redwoods in Humboldt County. For two years, she lived in that tree, which was 600 years old and stood 180 feet tall. The young woman, Julia "Butterfly" Hill, was protesting the Pacific Lumber Company's logging of the last of the redwood forests. Her civil disobedience attracted national media coverage and brought the redwood forests to the public's attention.

BY THE NUMBERS

California's Population

Estimates place California's 2006 population at 37,172,015, making it the country's most populated state, with 12 percent of all Americans calling it home. It is considered the country's 13th fastest-growing state, and it has about four million more residents than all of Canada.

Population Through the Years

Census Year	Population
1850	92,597
1860	379,994
1870	560,247
1880	864,694
1890	1,213,398
1900	1,485,053
1950	10,586,223
2000	33,871,648

Topping the Charts

Five of northern California's cities are listed in the country's 50 most populated cities. They are:

- San José, population 912,332, in 10th place
- San Francisco, population 739,426, in 14th place
- Fresno, population 461,116, in 37th place
- Sacramento, population 456,441, in 38th place
- Oakland, population 395,274, in 44th place

(By the way, New York is America's most populated city, with 8.1 million residents.)

Mother Tongue

The 2000 census points out that 61 percent of California residents speak English at home. Of the more than 200 languages spoken and read in California, Spanish is the second most popular language of choice, the pick of 26 percent of residents, and is considered the state's "alternative language." Chinese is the language of choice for three percent, Tagalog for three percent and Vietnamese for one percent of the population. California is considered one of the most linguistically diverse areas in the world.

Ethnic Diversity

According to the 2000 census, "less than half of Californians were white American or non-Hispanic white, the first recorded statistic (except for Hawaii) of a 'white minority' in any U.S. state." Here's what the overall population breakdown looks like, based on 2004 U.S. Census Bureau estimates:

Race	Percentage of Population
White (non-Hispanic)	44.5
Hispanic or Latino	34.7
Asian	12.1
Black American	6.8
Persons of two or more racial backgrounds	2.4
American Native/Alaskan Native	1.2
Native Hawaiian/Pacific Islander	0.4

Population Characteristics

California's population is fairly evenly divided when it comes to men and women. There are 16,996,756 women, equaling 50.2 percent of the population of the state, while men lag slightly behind at 16,874,892, or 49.8 percent. Most Californians fall in the 25 to 54 age range, with the average age being 33.3 years.

Overall Distribution

California's population per square mile is 217 persons.

With more than 3.8 million residents aged 65 and older, based on 2003 population estimates, California has the highest number of seniors of any state.

Will You Marry Me?

California has the largest number of residents older than 17 of any state—as of the 2000 census, more than 26 million. Of that number, 13.7 million were married at the time, 7.8 million had never been married, 2.5 million were divorced, 1.5 million were widowed, and 0.6 million were separated.

Religious Diversity

While New Age and eastern philosophies have gained notoriety in California, roughly 74 percent of residents still declare themselves Christians. Forty percent of residents are Protestant and 34 percent Catholic. Here's a closer look at the statistics:

Faith or Denomination	Percentage of California Population
Catholic	34
Baptist	8
Presbyterian	3
Methodist	2
Lutheran	2
Mormon	1
Other Protestant	23
Other Christian	3
Muslim	2
Jewish	2
Other Religious	3
Non-Religious	19

WHERE THE MONEY IS— AND WHERE IT ISN'T

Money Likes Money

If statistics are any indication, like tends to congregate with like. Northern California has among the highest average per capita annual income of just about anywhere on earth, while at the same time some of its residents earn among the lowest incomes of any First World country.

Wealthiest Northern California Cities

City	County	Average Income
Belvedere	Marin	$113,595
Atherton	San Mateo	$112,408
Woodside	San Mateo	$104,667

Poorest Northern California Cities

City	County	Average Income
Tobin	Plumas	$2584
Belden	Plumas	$3141
East Orosi	Tulare	$4984
London	Tulare	$5632
Cantua Creek	Fresno	$5693

ROADSIDE ATTRACTIONS

Cup of Joe?

Kingsburg's water tower is not only functional, it's also meant to be welcoming. The Kingsburg District Chamber of Commerce transformed the 60,000-gallon receptacle into a giant coffeepot in 1985. Its customized design, with its unique shape, floral emblem and color palette, reflects the town's Swedish heritage. You can even see the 122-foot-tall structure from Freeway 99. At night the tower is well lit, letting visitors and passersby know the coffee's always on!

Bonafante Gardens

Attention, all horticulture lovers. A trip to Bonafante Gardens in Gilroy provides a glimpse into the rare and odd when it comes to plant life on this planet.

Underground Escape

It began with a desire to escape the scorching heat of a Central Valley summer. Less than 20 years later, the underground labyrinth of intricate tunnels and grotto-like hideaways was turned into what is today the Forestiere Underground Gardens of Fresno.

Founder Baldassare Forestiere moved to the area from Sicily in 1906 as an enthusiastic 22-year-old who dreamed of farming. Discovering that the land he purchased was worthless for this venture, he began digging. By 1923, more than 10 acres had been hand-dug, and Forestiere was well on his way to creating an underground Mediterranean resort complete with the fruit trees and grapevines he'd hoped to grow above ground. Today, visitors can tour his underground world, where the ancient catacombs of Sicily have been recreated alongside courtyards and grottos, providing an escape from the heat into another reality.

TV Legends

What *Gunsmoke* enthusiast doesn't remember sheriff's deputy Festus Haggen? Why, there are still fan sites routinely searched on the Internet, even though the well-loved actor passed away in 1991. So it should be no surprise, then, that the town of Clovis—the town he called home—honored him by erecting a memorial statue, complete with hat, kerchief, gun and holster.

All You Want and More in a Store

If you stop by Casa de Fruita, chances are your youngsters will want to jump on the Casa de Carousel or Casa de Choo Choo. Since 1908, this family-owned fruit business has developed into a fully diversified, multi-dimensional enterprise that leaves most entrepreneurs in awe. Casa de Fruita first opened a roadside fruit market on Pacheco Pass Highway in Hollister back in 1940.

Since then, the family has added a restaurant, accommodations, theme-park-type attractions, regular community events and a wide array of goods for sale. Folks can even get hitched in Casa de Fruita Country Park! Talk about your one-stop shop.

Riding the Rails

It isn't an uncommon occurrence—a town springs up to support an industry or way of life, only to disappear once that industry is no longer viable. Such was the story of Laws. In 1883, the first train arrived at the railroad town built to accommodate it. In addition to its train station, agent's house and assorted other buildings required to meet the needs of regular train traffic, the town grew to have everything from a dance hall to a blacksmith shop. But when it became cheaper to use trucks to transport freight from neighboring mines, trains became redundant. The last whistle blew in Laws, located near Bishop, in 1960.

Buildings were rapidly demolished. Luckily, a few folks with foresight founded the Laws Museum, salvaging the depot, agent's house, oil and water tanks and turntable. Eventually other historic buildings were transported to the site, and today the remnants of a time gone by are preserved for visitors.

One Huge Statue

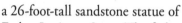

Sometime in history, folks in the Hillsboro area were really serious about honoring the founding father of one of their local Christian missions. If you're in the neighborhood and driving along Highway 280, also known as Junipero Serra Freeway, you'll immediately know what I mean. There, for all the world— and maybe even extraterrestrial life—to see is a 26-foot-tall sandstone statue of Father Junipero Serra. The father is on bended knee and pointing, though no one seems to be able to explain the significance of what exactly the good father is pointing to. In any case, the sight definitely turns heads.

Heaven on Earth

A little piece of heaven—it's just one way to describe the Alta Sierra Biblical Gardens in Grass Valley. It was as if Divine Providence directed John Sommer to this patch of land back in 1971. And he was quick to act on that direction, purchasing the property. Along with preserving its natural beauty, John re-created scenes from the Bible: a granite sculpture of Moses and the tablets, Jesus blessing the children, Jesus on the cross, Jesus raising from the dead. Sixteen statues dot a walking tour of the site, which visitors usually complete in 1.5 hours. Visitors can also tour a labyrinth, have a bite to eat in the picnic area and even plan a wedding or baptism at the site, which is run by a nonprofit, nondenominational organization.

Squash Galore!

There are many good reasons to stop by the city of Hayward, but the Zucchini Festival is certainly one of the most unusual ones. Calling itself the "Zucchini Capital of California," the city hosts this annual event on the third weekend in August, attracting more than 50,000 zucchini lovers. Together, folks celebrate the prolific produce in the form of all things zucchini—zucchini cake, zucchini jam, even zucchini ice cream. There are even zucchini carving contests and, of course, zucchini mascots—the Zucchini Rangers Zeek, Zack and Zuck.

Aviation History

There's no getting around it—war is a horrible thing. But there's something impressive about the planes flown in historic conflicts such as World War II. The Castle Air Museum, located in Atwater, boasts a collection of war planes like none other. The collection includes a B-17 Flying Fortress, a 1937 Douglas B-18 and a B-29 Super Fortress. With support from the United States Air Force Heritage Program, a group of interested folks in the Atwater-Merced area formed the not-for-profit Castle Air Museum Foundation Inc. in 1994, after the Castle Air Force Base was closed. At that time, the group assumed an existing collection of warplanes and built on it until today a total of 49 aircraft are on display.

DID YOU KNOW?

The folks down in Livermore claim they have the world's longest continuously burning lightbulb—it's been alight since 1901. Known as the Livermore Centennial Light, the only time it hasn't kept burning was during power outages and when it was being moved. After shining its light for more than 800,000 hours, the lightbulb has even made it into the *Guinness Book of World Records*. If you want to check it out, stop by the Livermore firehouse. Just a word of caution—it really doesn't look much different from a normal bulb.

One Long Bridge

For anyone who may share my phobia of bridges, this roadside attraction might best be traveled with your eyes closed—and someone else driving, of course. Some consider the covered bridge at Knights Ferry the longest covered bridge west of the Mississippi. Here are a few facts to chew on:

- Its 355-foot length spans the Stanislaus River.
- Uysses S. Grant, later a U.S. president, engineered it.
- Its construction in 1864 meant a ferry service was no longer required.
- It's the longest covered bridge in California.
- It's ranked as the ninth longest of its kind in theU.S.
- Originally, a toll was charged to those who wanted to cross: 2 cents per sheep or hog, $5 per horse or mule team, and $3 per elephant!

Memorial in Bronze

What better way to recognize a homegrown hero than with a statue in bronze? Located at the "Five Points" intersection in Modesto, a bronze statue of a teenaged couple sitting on the hood of a 1957 Chevy is a salute to Hollywood writer, producer, and director George Lucas and his 1973 movie *American Graffiti*.

Historic Home

Built in 1868, the Pardee Home on Eleventh Street in Oakland was transformed from a private home with collections and exhibits into a permanent museum in 1981. The building is as renowned for its architectural appeal as its contents are for their diversity. Among the interesting exhibits are Alaskan scrimshaw, Mexican rosaries, Californian-grown fine art and even an assortment of human skulls!

A Child's Paradise

Folks traveling through Oakland with youngsters in tow simply must stop by Children's Fairyland on Bellevue Avenue. The 10-acre park, created in the 1950s, breathes life into well-loved fairy tales with full-sized exhibits, interactive displays and even pint-sized costumes so youngsters can transform themselves into their favorite characters. As well, special events are held throughout the year, like the Jack O'Lantern Jamboree near Halloween.

The Sound of Water

San Francisco's Wave Organ is located in the city's Marina District. It is, basically, a wave-activated organ made up of an assortment of pipes inserted beneath a stone-and-concrete jetty. As water surges through the pipes at different times of the day with different levels of ferocity, visitors can hear a variety of different sounds. Peter Richards (an artist with the nearby Exploratorium) developed the idea for the parklike area and organ, and master sculptor and stonemason George Gonzales helped with its creation. The Wave Organ was completed in May 1986 and later dedicated to the memory of Frank Oppenheimer, the founding director of the Exploratorium.

Explore Your World

Making the world understandable to ordinary folk like you and me—that was Dr. Frank Oppenheimer's dream when he opened the doors of the Exploratorium in 1969. The interactive, experimental museum celebrating science, the arts and human perception is located in San Francisco's Palace of Fine Arts, near the Golden Gate Bridge. While it began with just a handful of exhibits, today there are about 650 on site.

Happy Camper, You Say?

Hiking enthusiasts will be happy to try out the trail to the Happy Camp Waterfalls. No, really. The trails in the area are beautiful, and the nearby community of Happy Camp is known to be quite friendly. Just one caution, though. This area is known for having one of the highest numbers of Bigfoot sightings in the world. Townsfolk have gone to great lengths to warn visitors of the fact by erecting a 15-foot-tall metal sculpture of the beast at the junction of Bigfoot and State of Jefferson byways.

History of a Different Kind

If you're into navy memorabilia and don't mind meeting up with a ghost or two, the USS *Hornet*, a floating museum in Alameda, will keep you looking over your shoulder. The aircraft carrier not only gives visitors a glimpse into navy history, it also gives them the opportunity to possibly meet up with one or two of the many ghosts believed to inhabit the vessel. Not unwilling to capitalize on an urban legend, museum curators here host an annual Monster Bash just before Halloween.

Wax Museums

The collection at the Wax Museum at Fisherman's Wharf, located on Jefferson Street in San Francisco, has tantalized visitors since 1962. Thomas L. Fong and his wife Eva founded the museum. Operating a wax museum in an historic structure was a far cry from life as Northern California's only garlic brokers. However, the couple was of an entrepreneurial spirit, and Thomas had always had his hand in a number of projects. He was involved in literally building the Bay Area community— apartments, buildings and even the 800-car Portsmouth Square Garage in Chinatown. Over the years, their Wax Museum has grown to include a number of specialty shops and—a prerequisite of sorts for wax museums everywhere—a Chamber of Horrors. In 1998, the historic building that once housed the museum was demolished, and a $15-million, 100,000-square-foot building was erected in its place. Today, the new museum boasts 250 figures from all areas of society: history, entertainment, sports, religion and more.

What's a Pez, Anyway?

For those of us who are not in the loop, the Museum of Pez
Memorabilia on California Drive in Burlingame might leave us
scratching our heads in wonder. Even some of us who are well
aware of what a Pez is may still wonder what all the fuss is
about. But maybe we should begin with a definition. A Pez is
a rectangular-shaped candy housed in a plastic dispenser decorated with a character head of some sort acting as the dispensing
portion. Move the head, and you'll be rewarded with a candy.

Edward Haas invented the Pez in Austria in 1927. The dispenser
was created for hygienic purposes in 1948, and the first Pez
plant in the U.S. was built in 1973 in Orange, Connecticut.
The first dispenser created was either the Full Body Santa or the
Full Body Robot. Today there are 300 different dispensers, and
chances are you can see or pick up a number of them from the
Museum of Pez Memorabilia. In 2004, the museum expanded
to include an exhibit of classic toys.

Good Old Faithful

Calistoga's Old Faithful is one of California's natural wonders and is one of three geysers in the world referred to as Old Faithful. They earn the name because of the regularity with which they spew hot water from the depths of the earth. In the case of Calistoga's Old Faithful, the eruption happens every 20 or 30 minutes.

Geysers are produced when hot magma heats water beneath the earth's surface to above the boiling point, sometimes as high as 350°. The geyser then spews a stream of hot water out of a hole in the ground. Water from Calistoga's Old Faithful shoots as high as 75 feet into the air.

One feature unique to the Calistoga geyser is that it can be used to predict oncoming earthquakes two to 14 days before the event—and with considerable accuracy. According to researchers, the underground tectonic stress that increases just before an earthquake affects the regularity of Old Faithful's eruptions, prolonging the time between events considerably. But if you check your watch and realize the day you're visiting is one of these occasions, don't fret. The predicted earthquake usually occurs about 500 miles down the road from the geyser.

Calistoga's Curiosities

Maybe it's because Calistoga is located in the mysterious and beautiful Napa Valley at the foot of Mount St. Helens, but Old Faithful isn't this community's only star attraction. Folks visiting here won't be at a loss for interesting activities.

☛ Hot-air balloon trips across the valley give visitors and residents alike a chance for an aerial view of the majestic countryside. Companies such as Balloons Above the Valley or Bonaventure Balloon Company Inc. charge in the neighborhood of $210 per person for the privilege.

☛ If you're interested in seeing how the other half lives and happen to be in Calistoga, check out Ca'Toga Galleria D'Arte on

Lincoln Avenue. The gallery features works of Italian-born classical artist Carlo Marchilori. For a more intimate look into the artist's life, a special tour of his home is held every Saturday.

- If you're into all things health-related, a trip to the Calistoga Mineral Water Company will afford a firsthand look at how nature's wonder in this neck of the woods is treated and bottled for your drinking pleasure.

- Calistoga's Petrified Forest is another natural wonder worth the visit. The privately owned park is actually a grove of petrified redwoods—trees that turned to stone. Originally, only the tips of these trees protruded from the earth's floor after the area was covered in a flow of volcanic ash. Natural erosion unearthed parts of the forest, and since 1871, people have worked to uncover the rest. Geologists consider the park to be one of the finest examples of a Pliocene fossil forest in the world.

- A short jaunt north of Calistoga on Highway 29 will bring you to Robert Louis Stevenson State Park. The park was named for the famed author after he chose the area to honeymoon with his bride back in 1880. According to the story, the couple lived in an old, abandoned mining bunkhouse for two months. What a treat!

- The Sharpsteen Museum features a wide collection of area memorabilia. The museum was the lovechild of Ben and Bernice Sharpsteen. The couple began the project when Ben retired from his career as an animator for Walt Disney Productions, and the finished product was donated to the city of Calistoga in 1978. Among the items on display is a collection of dioramas highlighting the history of the area. A special room is dedicated to the founder and includes information about his family and Hollywood history, including one of his Oscars.

- Animal lovers who want to explore the wild side will enjoy a visit to Safari West. The 400-acre sanctuary in the heart of California wine country is a haven to more than 400 species of African wildlife, all of which are endangered or extinct in their own natural habitat. Visitors have to drive with caution and stay

in their cars at all times. Even the cutest, most cuddly creature
can become dangerous when threatened.

☛ Calistoga is also famous for its mud baths. Spas in the town
offer a hot, gooey treat. I guess it's a treat, if you go in for that
sort of thing.

Cemetery Hunt

Folks who like to read headstones as a way of peeking into the
past might want to check out the Hills of Eternity Memorial
Park in Colma. That's where you'll find the headstone of outlaw
Wyatt Earp. Levi Strauss is also buried there.

DID YOU  KNOW?

Speaking of cemeteries, the town of Colma was chosen as the
site on which to establish area cemeteries after a California state
law, circa the late 1880s, was passed saying folks could no longer bury their dead on the family homestead or other undesig-
nated areas. By 1912, the town had 12 cemeteries. Unsanctioned
graveyards were dug up and the exhumed remains transported
to one of these sanctioned cemeteries. Those interested in cemetery walking can find numerous historic graves here. This could
be why some refer to Colma as the "City of the Dead."

Jelly Mania

If you've got a sweet tooth, a tour of the Jelly Belly Candy
Company in Fairfield will calm your craving. Founded in 1869,
this company produces more than 100 flavors of jellybeans and
was named the "Best Factory Tour in America" in a 2005
Reader's Digest article. If you do the tour, you'll no doubt agree
with the company's motto—they're definitely "more than just
a hill of beans."

New World Wonder

The Isis Oasis Sanctuary of Geyserville is a mecca of all things New Age. From its humble beginnings as an artists' studio and manufacturing center, Isis Oasis has evolved into a retreat center that offers everything from independent strolls to structured events.

Tunnel Tree

It's six feet wide and nine feet tall—just big enough for an average car to pass through. Believe it or not, that's exactly what it was built for! Back in the 1930s, Charlie and Hazel Underwood, along with help from a few foresters, carved this opening in a giant redwood nicknamed the Chandelier Tree. The tree, located in Underwood Park, a 200-acre redwood grove, got its name from its uniquely shaped branches. The Chandelier Tree is one of three such trees located on the Redwood Highway. If you're in the neighborhood south of Leggett, a visit is certainly in order.

Redwood Heaven

Touring California by car simply must include a drive through the Avenue of the Giants. The 31-mile drive through Humboldt County gives visitors a firsthand glimpse of these 2000-year-old monsters, which are only found in California and neighboring coastal regions. Just follow Old Highway 101 (which essentially parallels the new Highway 101) from Benbow to Fortuna. The trail is peppered with an assortment of natural attractions, including the 1500-year-old Chimney Tree, the Founders Tree, the Eternal Tree and the Immortal Tree.

Railway Luxury

While the ambiance could argue in its favor, it's a far cry from feeling like a hobo sleeping in an empty boxcar. In fact, the Napa Valley Railway Inn in Yountville is quite lovely. Retired boxcars and cabooses have been transformed into bedrooms and baths with a uniquely country feel. And, of course, these "rooms" are sitting on an original railway track!

Towering Tall

I stand 160 feet tall, weigh in at about 57,000 pounds, and was created from a 500-year-old redwood tree—what am I? Why, I'm the world's largest totem pole.

Created and carved by Ernest Pierson of Eureka in 1962 and erected in the McKinleyville Shopping Center's parking lot, the totem pole is likely one of the first things folks flying into McKinleyville see as they come in for a landing at the neighboring Arcata-Eureka Airport. Pierson calls the totem, which was created for the opening of the shopping center, a celebration pole.

Foster's Bighorn

Calamari Dore (steak) and Bighorn Bison Burgers might be as exotic fare as you can purchase at Foster's Bighorn, a restaurant on Main Street in Rio Vista—and it's likely a good thing, too! Should you be chowing down on moose meat, elk or antelope, you might find yourself a little put off by the 300 sets of doe eyes staring down at you from above. They are there because Foster's Bighorn is not only known for its grub, it's also known for its history. Bill Foster founded the bar-and-grill-type restaurant back in the early 1900s. An avid wildlife hunter, Bill made countless trips to Africa, Canada and Alaska, bringing home a trophy head from almost every trip. These, with his collection of photographs, have been mounted, preserved and hung as a testament to the beauty of the wild and as a call for preservation. (Ha! Some call, huh?)

The Muffler Man

There are about 180 Muffler Men in the U.S. These giant fiberglass mascots stand between 18 and 25 feet tall. With a few exceptions, each is a rendition of one of six basic models: a Native American, a cowboy, an astronaut, a lumberjack, a goofy-looking fella and an everyday, blue-collar Joe.

It's believed there may be an advertising link between the first Muffler Man and the hundreds scattered throughout America today, but it's a theory that's hard to prove. That first Muffler Man may have been erected as a mascot for mufflers and all-things exhaust-like, but the whole Muffler Man phenomenon has become just that, a phenomenon.

Giant Muffler Man–sized mascots litter roadways across the United States, and California is certainly no different. For example, an abandoned, giant-sized Native American warrior graces Alfred Harrell Highway. Also, a 10-foot-tall humanoid-looking figure made up of air-conditioning paraphernalia befit-tingly stands in front of the American Air, Heating and Air Conditioning building in Bakersfield.

DID YOU  KNOW?

Legend has it that the Hayward Giant, a.k.a. the Paul Bunyan Muffler Man, the Muffler Man on Mission Boulevard, Hayward, has been around for eons. At one point, his muffler was stolen. In its place he held a "work for food" sign. He's also been known to hold a scrub brush, a canoe paddle and even a full-grown woman!

MUST-SEE PLACES

"Look Up, Look Way Up"

While traveling Highway 101 North near Klamath, keep your eyes open for a must-see stop—and believe me, it won't be hard to find. A 49-foot-tall Paul Bunyan and a 35-foot-tall Babe the Blue Ox greet visitors to the Trees of Mystery site. Touted as the "premiere nature attraction on California's North Coast," an interpretive trail winds through a mile's worth of redwood forest, giving visitors an up-close and personal view of these botanical monsters. The site also offers gondola rides for folks who can't make the trail journey on foot.

Winchester Mystery House

It has 160 rooms, Tiffany art glass windows, parquet floors and 47 fireplaces. It sounds like a castle of historic proportions, but it began as the home of a grieving, albeit wealthy, widow. Sarah L. Winchester, heiress to the Winchester Rifle fortune, may have found herself at a loss after the death of her husband in 1884. She decided to start building a Victorian mansion that, by the time she died in 1922, had developed into a beautiful, if gargantuan, structure with more than its fair share of oddities. Among those strange twists of architecture are staircases that lead to solid ceilings, doors that open to walls and misshapen rooms of uninhabitable proportions. Located on South Winchester Boulevard in San José, the museum hosts a garden tour, mansion tour, behind-the-scenes tour to previously abandoned and unexplored areas of the house, and a tour of the Winchester Firearms Museum and Winchester Antique Products Museum. With the exception of Christmas, the museum is open every day, but visitors should call ahead for scheduled tour times.

DID YOU  KNOW?

In designing her mansion, Sarah L. Winchester never hired an architect. Instead, she drew her own plans on paper and, when paper wasn't close at hand, even on the odd tablecloth or two.

Pristine Condition

Ghost-town lovers will enjoy a stop at the Bodie State Historic Park, where a gold-mining boomtown still stands like a silent reminder of a time long past. By all accounts, the town stands intact. After its founding in the 1870s, the boom that led to Bodie's growth phased out. By 1962, the town had been turned over to the state in the hope it would be preserved. Today, more than 10,000 artifacts dating as far back as the 1870s are on display for the more than 200,000 visitors who stop by each year.

Mother-Daughter Lighthouse Keepers

In the early 1900s, two of northern California's lighthouses were "manned" by a mother and daughter. Emily Fish staffed the Point Pinos Lighthouse at the southern end of Monterey Bay, while her daughter, Juliet Nichols, kept the Angel Island Light and Fog Signal Station in San Francisco Bay.

The more famous of the two, Emily Fish served in her station for 20 years. She became known as the "Socialite Keeper" for the elegant style she maintained. Fish appointed the house with antique furniture and loved to entertain artists of the day as well as the passing naval officers. On the station's 92 acres, Fish kept French poodles and thoroughbred horses. Although she had refined tastes, Emily Fish was known for her skill and competence in her duties.

Say Gear-ar-delly

In 1837, a 20-year-old Italian man and his wife set sail from Italy for Uruguay. Little did Domenico (later changed to "Domingo") Ghirardelli know that he would become one of the world's most famous chocolatiers. After learning the trade in South America, Ghirardelli came to northern California to feed sweets to the hungry gold miners. From a tent in Stockton, he and his wife moved to a building in San Francisco. By 1866, Mrs. Ghirardelli & Co. was importing 1000 pounds of cocoa beans a year.

To help Americans pronounce the daunting name, the company printed a label on which a brightly colored parrot instructed consumers to "Say Gear-ar-delly."

In 1895, the company relocated to Ghirardelli Square, which was declared an official San Francisco city landmark in 1965 and is on the National Historic Register. It remains the site of the company's flagship store, the Ghirardelli Ice Cream and Chocolate Shop.

GHOSTLY ENCOUNTERS

Bad, Bad People

Gangsters and other shady characters were one-time visitors to the Brookdale Lodge in Brookdale, a scenic community of about 1000 people located in the Santa Cruz Mountains. The accommodation, in business since 1890, is believed to be haunted by several dozen ghosts. One urban legend has it that they are the disembodied spirits of bodies buried under the lodge's floorboards.

Don't Touch That

If visitors to the ghost town of Bodie take so much as a pebble home with them, they're sure to be cursed with very bad luck, indeed. Discovered in 1859, gold was the obvious draw for folks settling in the otherwise barren location. By 1880, there were as many as 10,000 people living in the town. The presence of a mind-boggling 60 saloons led to barroom brawls, murders and all manner of mayhem. Fires raged several times over the town's history—the 1932 fire destroyed as much as 95 percent of the town's buildings. By the end of World War II, the "Lucky Boy" mine was shut down. Only a handful of residents remained— six, to be exact. Of that number, five died horrible deaths and a ghost town was born. The site was named a state historic park in 1962. If you visit, be sure to leave empty-handed.

Apt Moniker

Legend has it Highway 152 near Gilroy, also known as Blood Alley, earned its name when a truck driver killed a woman. Her spirit is believed to wander the area, moaning and screaming, in search of her child.

Duck!

If you happen to visit Banta Inn, located in Banta, be prepared to duck on quick notice. That's because the ghost of its former owner, who died behind the bar in 1967, likes to toss objects from time to time.

Your Money's Worth and More?

A visit to the Moss Beach Distillery in Half Moon Bay might give you more than a full stomach. In fact, it might even scare your socks off! The ocean-view restaurant first opened in the 1920s, and it wasn't long before a chance encounter between a pretty patron and the bar's piano player turned into an historic event of paranormal proportions. Apparently, the beautiful lady, who always wore blue, frequented the establishment, unbeknownst to her husband and young son. An affair developed between the lovely lady and her piano man, but, as the story goes, the lady in blue died in a tragic car accident. Since that time, the Blue Ghost Lady has frequented the Moss Beach Distillery, searching for her long-lost love.

Paranormal investigators continue to study the ghost, and the story was even featured on the television series *Unsolved Mysteries*. With all this publicity, the owners of the establishment have admittedly played up the legend with high-tech illusions, swinging swag lamps and assorted extras. But stop by anyway—you might catch a glimpse of the real thing.

An Odd Place to Get Married (If You Ask Me)

One Northern California spot many couples choose to tie the knot is the Dunsmuir House, an elegant mansion in the East Bay. Fair enough…until you read up on the house's history.

Alexander Dunsmuir, son of a wealthy coal baron from British Columbia, had the house built in 1899 as a wedding gift for his fiancée, Josephine. The couple wed and went on their honeymoon in New York, where Alexander promptly died. Josephine came home to her new house, where she lived until her premature death in 1901.

The lavish enticements to encourage couples to hold their weddings at Dunsmuir House include the following phrase: "We want your wedding celebration to be filled with classic moments and memories that last a lifetime." I would add, "however short it might be."

THE WHEN AND HOW OF NORTHERN CALIFORNIA'S COMMUNITIES

Sacramento

When two Spanish soldiers wandered over from Mission San José in 1808, they were the first recorded Europeans in what today is the Sacramento Valley. It wasn't until 1839, however, that a Swiss immigrant named Captain John Augustus Sutter homesteaded the area. Receiving a land grant from the Mexican government, Sutter developed an agricultural estate he named New Helvetia, meaning "New Switzerland." This estate, also called Sutter's Fort, later became the city of Sacramento. The city was named California's permanent state capital in 1854.

DID YOU KNOW?

The ill-fated Donner Party's survivors were rescued by relief parties from Captain John Augustus Sutter's farm in what is today Sacramento.

San Francisco

San Francisco was first established as a Mexican mission, in 1776, five days before the Declaration of Independence. Lieutenant José Joaquin Moraga led a group of colonists and soldiers north from the Mexican state capital of Monterey Presidio and founded the Mission Dolores and the city of San Francisco de Asís.

DID YOU KNOW?

In March 1848, a few months before the Gold Rush began, San Francisco (California's largest population center at the time) had an estimated European population of 812. Within two years, that number had risen to 100,000.

Monterey

In 1602, Sebastian Vizcaino of Spain was the first European to set foot on what would later become Monterey. The town was officially founded in 1770. It served as the Mexican state capital of California and, after the Mexican-American War, hosted the American state's founding constitutional convention.

San José

Founded in 1777, San José is the oldest civil settlement in California. Before the Spaniards came, 40 tribes of Native Americans who called themselves the Ohlone (meaning "abalone people") inhabited the area. The city, which was incorporated in 1850, is now the third largest city in California and serves as the Santa Clara county seat.

CLASSIC CALIFORNIA

Before it gained a reputation as the nation's high-tech innovation center, San José was famous for its fruit orchards, canneries and ranches.

Eureka

There is evidence to suggest that the Humboldt County area was first visited by people from another land in 217 BC, when a Chinese junk captain named Hee-li mistakenly wound up there. Other evidence indicates that Chinese sailors also crossed the Pacific around 485 AD. But it wasn't until the 1849 gold rush that outsiders settled in the area. That year, Dr. Josiah Gregg and his six companions arrived overland along the Eel River. The Mendocino Exploration Company established the town of Eureka the following year. Nearby Arcata (at first called Union) was established that same year by the Union Company.

Fresno

With miners flocking through the Central Valley, it was just a matter of time before some of them settled the area. In 1860, Fresno County listed its population as "4304 whites, 305 Chinese and 3294 Indians." It wasn't until the Central (later Southern) Pacific Railroad put up a station there in 1872 that the town of Fresno was born.

DID YOU KNOW?

In 1863, during the Civil War, Union troops were stationed at Fort Miller to keep it in Union hands.

FOUNDING FATHERS (AND MOTHERS)

The Indigenous People

Of course before any of the Spanish, English, Russians or French showed up, there were Native Americans living here. In the northwest region of the state lived the Yurok, Hupa and Shasta tribes; in the northeast were the Achumawi and Atsugewi peoples; and the central region was home to the Pomo, Miwok, Maidu and Yokuts tribes.

Sir Francis Drake

This pirate, commissioned by his rumored squeeze Queen Elizabeth I of England in 1577 to pillage and reap (yes, "reap") gold and other booty from Spanish ships, landed on the California coast in 1579. Accounts of the day say that he had to come ashore for repairs because his ship's holds were literally bursting with the ill-gotten loot.

DID YOU  KNOW?

No one knows the exact location where Sir Francis Drake landed in 1579. To show he meant business, he put up a brass plate claiming California for England, saying "this kingdome... to be knowne unto all men as Nova Albion." This plaque has never been found, though a prank-inspired imitation was discovered near San Francisco in the 1930s. It was believed authentic until the brass was age-tested in 1977. Recently, archaeologists discovered what they believe to be the remains of a fort that Drake built on the west shore of Bolinas Lagoon.

Father Junipero Serra

A Spanish Franciscan clergyman, Junipero Serra, arrived in Alta California (as opposed to Baja California, meaning "lower California") in 1769. He established California's first nine missions and served as father/president of the mission system. The missions had the twofold purpose of converting the Native American population to Catholicism and extending Spain's territory. Historical records say that Native Americans worked in the missions under oppressive conditions, to which they responded by slowing work, running away and, in some cases, revolting violently. Recently, the pope beatified Junipero Serra, the second step towards sainthood. The padre's critics object, calling him a sadist and a fanatic for his treatment of Native Americans.

DID YOU  KNOW?

Some of the Native Americans in northwestern California determined a family's status by its possession of conspicuous objects of wealth, such as white deerskins, tubular mollusk shells and the ever-popular woodpecker scalps.

John C. Frémont

Frémont was a busy guy, the sort who's hard to categorize. One day (June 14, 1846, to be exact), during the Bear Flag Revolt, he was throwing upstanding citizens, such as Colonel Mariano Guadalupe Vallejo, in chains and declaring California a free republic; another time (1848) he was court-martialed for mutiny and disobedience and found guilty, and before you know it (1850), he was selected to represent California in the U.S. Senate. Go figure.

DID YOU  KNOW?

Abraham Lincoln's nephew made the first California flag. William Todd made a flag with a star and what was supposed to be a grizzly bear—though it looks a lot more like a pig—on it.

Mary Ellen (Mammy) Pleasant

Former slave Mary Ellen "Mammy" Pleasant came to San Francisco from the East Coast around 1849. As the owner of boarding houses and a ring of fancy prostitutes, Pleasant acquired great wealth and power in the burgeoning city. She earned the title of the "Mother of Civil Rights in California" by helping win rights for black people to testify in court, ride streetcars and earn respectable wages. Before slavery was outlawed, she helped thousands of freed slaves escape into Canada, giving her the reputation as the "western terminus" of the Underground Railroad. She is even rumored to have helped finance John Brown's ill-fated raid on Harper's Ferry.

DID YOU  KNOW?

California was the first American state to allow a married woman to maintain ownership of her own property, whether acquired before marriage or during. This right was included in the original 1849 state constitution. The law followed the Mexican California tradition but was unheard of in the U.S.

John Muir

When he arrived in northern California in 1868, naturalist John Muir promptly fell in love with the Sierra Nevada Mountains and dedicated his life to protecting them. In 1890, Muir succeeded in getting Yosemite established as a national park. In 1892, he founded the Sierra Club in order to preserve other natural treasures.

NOTABLE EVENTS

Sir Francis Drake Stepped Ashore: June 17, 1579

Sir Francis Drake probably first stepped ashore on the Point Reyes Peninsula. The Native Americans there greeted him in a way to which the Englishman was not accustomed. A group of Miwok placed a feathered crown on Drake's head, and, as Drake's journals record, they wailed and scratched their cheeks. Drake assumed that these humble folk were crowning him king, acceding their lands to him (not sure how he came up with that, but never mind) and believed he and his crew to be gods. The guy had serious narcissism issues, but there were no therapists around yet to diagnose him. Study of Miwok customs show that the gestures were likely those of mourning. It is most likely that Drake's welcoming party mistook him for a ghost returning from the afterlife.

Cannibalism: 1846

The Donner Party, led by George Donner, attempted to cross the Sierra Nevadas in the winter of 1846 but got stopped by the heaviest snowfall in 30 years—more than 20 feet. Only 47 of the original 87 travelers survived. Some did so by eating other members of the group. In order to be sure we all remember this uplifting event, two places in the area where the group met their misfortune were named after them, Donner Lake and Donner Pass.

"25 Women Arrived on Different Vessels Today"
So read a San Francisco newspaper headline on December 20, 1849. Hey, it was a big event!

The First "Public" Transit

The earliest people from other lands arrived in California by ship. The first people to pay for transport into the state by land took the Butterfield stage on its 2800-mile route from Missouri in 1858.

All the Comforts of a Stagecoach

One of America's foremost authors, Samuel Clemens, better known as Mark Twain, had the so-called pleasure of taking an early stagecoach into California. As a young man, Twain traveled west in 1864 to take a job at the *Golden Era* newspaper in San Francisco. He described the trip in a characteristically droll manner:

> *Whenever the stage stopped to change horses, we would wake up, and try to recollect where we were....We began to get into country, now, threaded here and there with little streams. These had high, steep banks on each side, and every time we flew down one bank and scrambled up the other, our party inside got mixed somewhat.*
>
> *First we would all be down in a pile at the forward end of the stage, nearly in a sitting posture, and in a second we would shoot to the other end, and stand on our heads. And we would sprawl and kick, too, and ward off ends and corners of mailbags that came lumbering after us and about us; and as the dust rose from the tumult, we would all sneeze in chorus, and the majority of us would grumble, and probably say some hasty thing like "Take your elbow out of my ribs! Can't you quit crowding."*

First Mail Service

The first mail service to San Francisco began in 1847. Two soldiers on horseback, riding by way of San Diego, brought mail. Regular mail service first reached the interior of the state, with stops at Benicia, Sacramento and San José, in 1849.

DID YOU  KNOW?

One quarter of the gold miners in northern California in 1870 were Chinese.

$1 Train Trip

In 1886, you could buy a train ticket from Kansas City to Los Angeles for only $1. The "Railroad Wars" were in full swing that year, and the lines competed hotly for travelers' business.

The Great San Francisco Earthquake: 5:12 AM, April 18, 1906

A series of quakes hit northern California, the largest of them estimated at 8.3 on the Richter scale. Buildings collapsed and gas mains snapped, causing fires throughout the city. Some of the fires burned at temperatures estimated to be as high as 2000°. The disaster leveled four square miles of the city (490 blocks), and as many as 3000 people died.

The Worst Terrorist Act in San Francisco History: 1916

The Preparedness Day Bombing of 1916, the worst terrorist act in San Francisco history, took place on July 22, 1916, as the city held a parade in anticipation of the nation joining World War I. Half an hour after the parade began, a bomb in a suitcase exploded near the Ferry Building, killing 10 bystanders and wounding 40 others. Two radical labor leaders, Thomas Mooney and Warren K. Billings, were arrested, hastily tried and, in spite of a lack of evidence, sentenced to life in prison. In 1939, after investigations revealed rampant perjury and false evidence, both men were pardoned. The true bomber was never found.

California was a colonial province of Spain from 1769 to 1821. From 1821 to 1848, California belonged to Mexico.

The First Wagon Train Crossed the Sierras: 1841
John Bidwell led a group of early California pioneers who settled in what became Chico.

DID YOU KNOW?

In the early days of California's statehood, the northernmost reaches of the state were considered especially dangerous. Referring to two rivers in the Eureka area, the saying went, "There is no law north of the Eel and no God north of the Klamath."

California's Original State Flag was First Raised: June 14, 1846
A group of rebels claimed California as a free nation in the "Bear Flag Revolt."

Gold Was Discovered at Sutter's Mill: January 24, 1848
Although California was Mexican territory at the time, it became U.S. territory only two days later, a move that was unrelated to the fortuitous discovery. (Yeah, sure!)

DID YOU KNOW?

The man on whose land gold was first discovered in California, John Sutter, was eventually forced from his land and died bankrupt as a result of the gold rush that ensued.

A Star Was Stitched onto the U.S. Flag: September 9, 1850
California was admitted as a U.S. state.

Depression & the Dust Bowl: 1930s

Hard times in Oklahoma, Texas and Arkansas brought the
"Okies" to California. These farming families sought a brighter
future after dust storms wiped out their farms.

The San Francisco General Strike: 1934

On "Bloody Thursday" (July 5, 1934), 64 strikers were injured
and two were killed. In response, nearly every union in San
Francisco and Alameda counties went on strike, bringing the
city grinding to a halt for four days.

WARS AND CONFLICT

The Jones Incident of 1842

In an embarrassing moment in California history, Commodore Thomas Catesby Jones of the U.S. Marines was stationed off the coast of California, when he heard a rumor that the U.S. and Mexico were at war. Jones hurried ashore with his troops and triumphantly claimed the capital city of Monterey, running the U.S. flag up the flagpole. Unfortunately for Jones, the rumor was false. He quietly sent his troops back to the ship and sailed away.

The Bear Flag Revolt, June 14, 1846

Lieutenant John C. Frémont, an officer in the Army Corps of Topographical Engineers, had no authorization to start a war. Nevertheless, along with 60 other armed men, he arrived in Mexican California in 1846 looking for a fight. He and a group of Anglo-Americans captured Colonel Mariano Guadalupe Vallejo in his hometown of Sonoma and proclaimed themselves an independent republic. The California Republic had a short life, ending in July of the same year, when U.S. forces ousted Frémont's crew.

DID YOU KNOW?

California's admission as a state upset the balance in Congress between free and slaveholder states. This created a huge controversy and almost prevented statehood. California was always an anti-slavery state. The vote for a free state was unanimous at the first Constitutional Convention. Approval for statehood only went through when a strict fugitive slave bill mollified Southern senators.

Mexican American War, 1846–48

Four years after the Jones Incident prematurely claimed California as U.S. territory, following the Bear Flag Revolt, U.S. troops did invade California and claim the territory. The war ended with the signing of the Treaty of Guadalupe Hidalgo in 1848. In the treaty, Mexico gave up fully half of its territory.

UNIQUE PLACES

A Jewish Agricultural Colony

In 1888, the town of Orangevale (now a suburb of Sacramento) was founded as an agricultural colony for Jewish immigrants, many of whom had fled pogroms in Eastern Europe. California dry-goods merchant Harris Weinstock decided to market 10-acre farmsteads in Orangevale to the new Jewish immigrants. The colony didn't flourish, possibly because the new arrivals came from cities and lacked agricultural skills.

DID YOU KNOW?

During California's Gold Rush, the small town of Fiddletown in Amador County boasted the largest number of Chinese settlers—around 2000—of any place in the U.S. outside San Francisco.

The Dream of Allensworth

Allensworth, just north of Bakersfield, was the only California town founded, financed and governed by an African American. Lieutenant Colonel Allen Allensworth founded Allensworth in an attempt to create a town where black citizens could live free of racial discrimination. When the founder died unexpectedly in 1914, the town's residents drifted away. Today a state historical park commemorates Allensworth's dream.

Rollin' in the Dough?

Marin County ranks as the richest county in the nation with a median household income (in 2000) of $71,306. The city of Belvedere, in Marin County, is the richest city in the state.

According to U.S. census figures, residents in Belvedere make a median of more than $113,000 each.

On the other hand, there's the town (or "census designated place") of Tobin, with a population of 11, where residents rake in a humble $2584 per year on average.

Pretty Ugly

Sam, the winner of Petaluma's Ugly Dog Contest for three years running, is credited with breaking up his owner's relationship... and then turning around and playing cupid. According to the dog's owner, Susie Lockheed, when she rescued the pooch, her boyfriend found the little critter so offensive that he broke up with her. Good riddance to bad rubbish, I say. The real Romeo came onto the scene when he saw a picture of Sam (along with Susie, presumably) on a dating site and fell for them both.

Got Humboldt?

Napa County is famous for wine. Humboldt County is famous for its own type of relaxing, recreational substance—the green, resinous variety. Remote areas of Humboldt appealed to pot growers who moved north from the Bay Area after the more relaxed 1970s evolved into the "War on Drugs."

In 1983, the Feds caught on and attached a special Marijuana Eradication Unit to the Humboldt County Sheriff's Department. In 2002, the largest indoor marijuana-growing bust in California history took place in Humboldt when police seized 12,000 plants and handed the growers 20-year prison sentences. Before the bust, the growers were estimated to be making $50,000 a month. Not bad for a gardener.

PLACE NAMES

Fiddletown

Fiddletown, located in Amador County, was originally named in 1853. According to most sources, it received its name from the Missourians who settled and mined in the area. In 1878, the name didn't sit well with one townsman, who reportedly didn't think it dignified to be known as "a man from Fiddletown." By all reports, he lobbied for the name to be changed to Oleta after his daughter and was successful in his attempts. The new name remained until the name-changing advocate died in 1932, and residents lobbied to revert back to the original name.

Whiskey Creek

Once upon a time, a gold prospector was swimming his pack mules across a creek. When he was halfway across, a keg of whiskey came loose and washed away. In those days, a keg of whiskey was worth 50 mules, or so the man lamented loudly. In his moment of anguish, the prospector named the creek for his lost goods.

DID YOU  KNOW?

The community of Oregon House started out in 1850 as little more than a log cabin. Two years later, a hotel was built and named Oregon House. Before long, the growing community adopted the name, and today Oregon House boasts a population of between 1500 and 3000 people—depending on whether you want to listen to the statisticians or the residents!

You Bet

Around 1857, Lazarus Beard, a saloon owner in the Sierra foothills of Nevada County, wanted a name for the mining town growing up around his saloon. Beard offered his customers a steady supply of whiskey, to keep the old gears turning to think up a good name. No fools they, the customers had no intention of messing with a good thing—as long as they offered names sure to fail, the whiskey kept flowing.

One day, one of the drinkers offered a ridiculous option, hoping to keep the game going. Unfortunately for the partiers, Beard loved the name. The town was dubbed You Bet, and everyone had to go home and sober up.

Lake Tahoe Tug-of-War

Early American settlers fought over what to name (or actually rename, since the Native Americans had named the lake long before) Lake Tahoe. "Tahoe" derives from the local Washoe word *da'aw*, meaning "lake" or "big water." Some maps from 1848 record the name Lake Bonpland, given by explorer John Frémont to honor French botanist Aimé Bonpland. In 1854, friends of Governor John Bigler put their stamp on the lake, renaming it Lake Bigler. However, Bigler's outspoken support of Southern secession during the Civil War turned popular sentiment against him, and people reverted to using the original Washoe name.

Bigler's supporters threw a legislative fit and passed an act of California Congress in 1870 stating that (by gosh) the official name was Lake Bigler. The public ignored them. The name Tahoe became so widely used that in 1945, when the state congress finally relented and changed the official name to Tahoe, no one knew what they were talking about.

Berkeley

Oddly, Berkeley, a city known for its wild 1960s cultural revolution and free-thinking culture, was named after an Anglican bishop who not only never stepped foot on the West Coast, but also wrote tracts against free-thinking.

Then again, as one of the most famous 18th-century British Empiricists (along with Hume and Locke), George Berkeley believed that physical objects are made up entirely of thought. Hmm, okay. Those theories would have fit right in with latter-day LSD evangelist (and Berkeley prof) Timothy Leary and friends, so maybe the name's more apt than it appears.

Calaveras County

"Calaveras" comes from the Spanish word meaning "skulls." This is said to refer to the bones in the area that were found after a Native American war.

Sonoma County

The best sources say *sonoma* translates (from either the local Chocuyen language or from Italian) as the poetic "Valley of the Moon," but there are dissenters who insist that it means "Land of the Tribe of Chief Nose." (Maybe the Chocuyen chief in the area had a big honker.)

NOTABLE HAPPENINGS

The Wakamatsu Tea and Silk Farm

In 1869, a group of refugees fled political upheaval in Japan and came to the California Gold Country. The settlers brought mulberry trees, silkworm cocoons, bamboo shoots and tea plants in hopes of establishing an agricultural settlement in what is now Coloma. The silk and tea farming failed because of a variety of factors, including an inadequate water supply. The Marshall Gold Discovery State Historic Park today has a few relics left by this group of early settlers, including a Japanese sword and a banner bearing the crest of the Aizu Wakamatsu clan.

The Valley That Built L.A.

William Mulholland of Los Angeles decided in the early 1900s that if the City of Angels was to prosper, it would need lots of water. Mulholland started (by hook and by crook, it's said) acquiring water rights to the rich Owens Valley in the south of Northern California.

The aqueduct bringing Owens Valley water to the city was completed in 1913. But, before it was, outraged Owens Valley farmers, who felt they'd been tricked out of their water, fought back. Someone (he/they who must not be named) dynamited the aqueduct 14 times during its construction.

As a result of the aqueduct, by 1924, Owens Lake (once 15 miles long and 30 feet deep) and 50 miles of the Owens River were dry as a bone.

Pipe City

In the 1930s, some of the many people left homeless by the Depression's hard times found homes in six-foot-long sections of huge cement pipe that sat above ground in Oakland. The 200 inhabitants covered the open pipe ends with burlap or cardboard to keep out the wind and lived on mulligan stew made from produce scavenged from the nearby grocery wholesalers' garbage cans. The pipe-dwellers called it "Miseryville," but the press dubbed the spot "Pipe City."

DID YOU  KNOW?

A samurai warrior is buried in the Pioneer Cemetery in Coloma. He was probably one of the Japanese immigrants who settled around Placerville in the 1860s.

A Park for the People

In April 1969, a group of Berkeley residents banded together, planting flowers and building children's play areas, to turn an empty piece of university land into a park. The community enjoyed their newly created park for three weeks before the university called in 100 California Highway Patrol officers to bulldoze the gardens and erect a cyclone fence around the site.

Enraged, 3000 protesters flooded the streets around the closed park. Violence erupted. Rocks flew, and tear-gas filled the air. After several days of upheaval, Governor Ronald Reagan sent in 2000 National Guard troops. The National Guard occupied the city for weeks. By the end of the fracas, 120 people had been injured, one blinded and one killed.

After the violence, the university and the city came to a tentative agreement: informally, the People's Park is open to the public, though the land still belongs to the university.

Summer of Love

John Phillips of the band The Mamas and The Papas penned a song that became the anthem for the summer of 1967 and for the many tumultuous years that followed: "If you're going to San Francisco, be sure to wear some flowers in your hair..." (Scott McKenzie's version of the song topped the 1967 charts.) Thousands of young people from across the country did just that. With flowers in their hair, they descended on San Francisco's Haight-Ashbury district and launched the hippie generation.

It was definitely sex, drugs and rock 'n' roll. The list of bands in town that summer reads like a who's who of early rock, including The Grateful Dead, Jefferson Airplane and Big Brother and The Holding Company (Janis Joplin's band). But it was an idealistic version, one inspired by peaceful war resistance and, for many, a desire to "expand" their minds with psychedelics.

CLAIM TO FAME

The Home of Rosie the Riveter

Rosie the Riveter, that icon of American World War II (and especially women's) can-do attitude, came from Richmond. In 1941, with the war on, the city's deep-water port and exposed shoreline caught the eye of shipbuilder Henry Kaiser. With so many men overseas fighting, Kaiser turned to local women to staff the shipyards. The women stepped up and...well, riveted and welded and operated heavy equipment. The press of the day called them "Rosie the Riveters."

The shipyards also sought employees in the American South. With the influx of those former sharecroppers, the area's African-American population increased. These newly trained men and women built ships at a dizzying pace, completing 747 Liberty and Victory ships by the war's end. The Liberty ship *Robert E. Peary*, which Richmond workers built in just over four days, set a world record that has still not been surpassed.

You're a Good Man, Charles Schulz

The creator of the world-famous *Peanuts* comic strip called Sonoma County his home. Charles Schulz moved from Minnesota to Sebastopol with his wife and five children in 1958 and then to nearby Santa Rosa in 1969, where he opened the Redwood Empire Ice Arena. Schulz passed away in Santa Rosa in 2000.

Charlie Brown and friends inspired the first-ever animated television special, the award-winning *A Charlie Brown Christmas*, in 1965, and accompanied astronauts on the Apollo X mission. After showing up in their 2000th newspaper in 1984, they even earned a place in the *Guinness Book of World Records*.

DID YOU  KNOW?

Peanuts comic-strip creator Charles Schulz, long-time resident of Sonoma County, is one of the best-paid dead people around. With millions of dollars per year flowing into his estate, according to *Forbes Magazine*, Schulz's posthumous earning power is topped only by Kurt Cobain and Elvis Presley.

Three Little Pigs' Lesson

In 1852, the city of Sacramento learned a hard lesson, the same one the three little pigs learned—bricks are tougher than sticks. That year, a terrible fire destroyed more than 85 percent of the city. After the disaster, buildings were rebuilt with brick rather than wood.

Crème de l'Auto

Pebble Beach Golf Links holds what is reputedly the most prestigious classic and vintage car show in the country. Sleek autos at the Pebble Beach Concours d'Elegance (French for a "competition of elegance"—ooh-la-la) are judged on function, originality and presentation. Now, *where* did I set my champagne, dah-ling?

Do You Know the Way To...

Superstar Dionne Warwick crooned the city to fame in her 1968 Grammy-Award-winning performance of "Do You Know the Way to San José?" which also went to number 10 on the U.S. charts (and number eight in Britain). The lyrics tell of a woman grown tired of the pace of Los Angeles who longs to go home to San José. Word has it that Hal David, who co-wrote the song with Burt Bacharach, grew fond of the sunny central California city while stationed there with the navy.

The Ugliest Dog

The town of Petaluma, about an hour north of San Francisco, has several quirky claims to fame. At the turn of the last century, with poultry as its main industry, Petaluma proudly flaunted the title of "Chicken Capital of the World." Some know it for the Polly Klaus tragedy or as the home of the World Wristwrestling Championships, but the town may be best known for its ugly pooches.

Each year, Petaluma hosts the Ugly Dog Contest, during the county's Sonoma-Marin Fair. A snaggle-toothed, hairless (but nevertheless pedigreed) Chinese crested named Sam stole the show three years in a row starting in 2003, earning himself numerous TV appearances and even a howdy-do with millionaire Donald Trump (no beauty himself, as dogs go).

DID YOU KNOW?

The town of Martinez is proud to be the birthplace of Joe DiMaggio. Whether he was in centerfield or at bat, Hall of Famer DiMaggio was one of the game's most graceful athletes.

LIFE IN NORTHERN CALIFORNIA

Ropin' and Ridin'

What people in other parts often don't realize about Northern California is that the beach-and-surfer and granola-munching-hippie images are just a small percentage of what the state is really about. A bunch of us are rural, agricultural folks.

The weeklong Fortuna Rodeo, started in 1921, is the oldest rodeo in northern California, boasting the largest payoff per event in the state. Fun-loving rodeo-goers won't want to miss the greased-pole climb or the ever-popular cow-chip throwing contest. (You use what's on hand.) What's more, each year, an unsuspecting couple gets "kidnapped" and treated to several days of luxurious lodgings and food, before getting to ride in the rodeo parade—in the "Kidnapped Tourists" place of honor.

That Mind-Body Integration Thing

Nearly 200 miles south of San Francisco in Big Sur sits one of Northern California's oldest retreat centers geared towards "inner work," offering courses in cleansing your chakras, tuning up a lesbian relationship and improving your love life. (At least, I think that's what "The Intimate Couple: An Integrative Body Psychotherapy Workshop" is about.)

Founded in 1962, Esalen has hosted a stream of mind-body teachers and out-of-the-box thinkers, including Aldous Huxley (Mr. *Brave New World*), gonzo journalist Hunter S. Thompson, mythologist Joseph Campbell, Fritz Perls (papa of Gestalt ther-apy) and self-actualizer Abraham Maslow. Currently, about 10,000 people a year show up to relax in the natural hot springs, get a massage and take a peek inside themselves.

Each of the more than 30,000 attendees of the 1967 "Human Be-In" in Golden Gate Park—featuring speakers Jerry Rubin, Allen Ginsberg and Timothy Leary as well as music by The Grateful Dead and Jefferson Airplane—was advised to bring beads, bells, costumes, feathers, cymbals, flags and, of course, flowers to share.

Nude Beaches

In 1972, a California court case set the precedent that going butt-naked on a beach does not necessarily constitute indecent exposure. What has evolved in the state is a number of sites (mostly unofficial) where you can take it all off.

The only state-designated "clothing-optional beach" is Gray Whale Cove State Beach near Pacifica. It was formerly known as "Devil's Slide," which better fits the slippery slope associated with such libertine behavior. A private beach in San Gregorio, south of Half Moon Bay, claims to be the oldest nude beach in California, with a start date of 1967. Don't confuse this spot with San Gregorio State Beach, where you will get ticketed for dropping trow.

If you like to do more in the buff than just laze around, you can participate in San Francisco's Naked Yoga Sports Day or help the Bay Area Naturists (a.k.a. BAN) clean up Santa Cruz's Bonny Doon Beach. (Personally, I think I would miss having pockets.)

The Great Outdoors

Northern Californians, whether city or country dwellers, are an outdoorsy bunch. Seventy percent of all those polled recently had participated in some kind of outdoor recreation in the last year.

City folk preferred day hiking, camping, fishing and looking at wildlife, while rural residents, on their outings, were more likely to hop on a horse or an ORV (off-road vehicle) or to go hunting.

Ecotourism

In 1992, "ecotourism" generated about $9.9 billion throughout California, while in the northern coastal counties of San Mateo, Santa Cruz and Monterey, it took in $63.2 million (in 1988). "Green" activities include bird watching, tide pooling, whale watching and hiking.

Jet Skis

Since they were introduced in 1974, jet skis sales have taken off in California. In 1994, jet skis made up half of all the recreational boat sales in the state, and there are currently more than 91,000 of them registered in California.

Recreational Diving

Recreational diving in northern California increased by 10 to 20 percent in the 1980s and six percent in the 1990s. The sport brought in $14 million for central coast dive shops. The Northern California Diver's Association estimated that 70 percent of north coast dives took place in Monterey Bay.

Fishing for Fun

Along the Northern California coast (from San Luis Obispo to Humboldt County), recreational fishing has increased 65 percent from 1960 to 1985. Catch by weight almost doubled in that same period.

Mall Rats

Okay, not everyone in the Golden State is out in the hills, hiking. A lot of them are shopping. There are at least 6000 malls in the state, giving California the most malls in the nation. In terms of per capita numbers, we're down at number 18, with only two malls for every 10,000 shoppers. Taking top mall honors for Northern California (based on accessibility, cleanliness, etc.) are the Westfield Valley Fair Mall in San José, Palo Alto's Stanford Shopping Center and Westfield San Francisco Centre.

A Day at the Museum

According to the USA Museum Database, there are 74 museums in Northern California, examining everything from wine (in Napa, of course) to Pez memorabilia, from aircraft carriers to Japanese art.

Dinner Out

California has about 2.5 restaurants for every 1000 people. Last year, Golden Staters spent $51.5 billion eating out.

Ride the Giant Dipper

Northern California is home to the oldest amusement park in the state and the only one situated on the Pacific Ocean. The Santa Cruz Boardwalk also boasts two National Historic Landmarks—the gorgeous 1911 Looff Carousel and the 1924 Giant Dipper roller coaster.

DRUGS, BOOZE AND ALL THINGS NAUGHTY

The Elixir of Quietude

What work of art inspired H.L. Mencken to call it "the only American invention as perfect as the sonnet" and E.B. White to dub it "the elixir of quietude"? Why, the martini, of course. And there's evidence that it may have been invented in Northern California.

According to one account, a prospector set a gold nugget on the bar of San Francisco's Occidental Hotel in the 1850s. He was headed for the town of Martinez, across the bay some 30 miles, and needed something to ease his journey. The barman, Jerry Thomas, mixed him a brew and published his recipe later in the 1887 *Bartender's Guide* as follows: "Use small bar glass, one dash bitters, two dashes Maraschino, one wineglass of vermouth, two small lumps of ice, one pony of Old Tom gin, SHAKE up thoroughly, and strain into a large cocktail glass. Put a quarter of a slice of lemon in the glass, and serve. *If the guest prefers it very sweet, add two dashes of gum syrup.*" (Emphasis his.)

Given that Old Tom was a sweetened gin, add the maraschino and you have…well, a grossly sweet version of the modern martini, but a version all the same. Thomas supposedly named the drink after the customer's destination, "The Martinez."

The town of Martinez likes to think that the prospector was headed the other way. There's a plaque in the town commemorating the day in the 1870s when Martinez saloon owner Julio Richelieu mixed up what they say was the first martini.

Flesh at the World's Fair

The 1939 Treasure Island World's Fair featured an amusement zone known as the "Gayway" that, while not "gay" by modern usage, did shock more than a few straightlaced fair-goers. One of the most popular exhibits was, according to the official Fair guidebook, "Sally Rand Nude Ranch: A dude ranch á la 1939," in which dancer Sally Rand and her fellow cowgirls wore hats and boots but little in between.

After her Treasure Island exhibit, Sally opened the Music Box Nightclub (now the Great American Music Hall) in the Polk Gulch area of San Francisco, where she was famous for her sexy fan dances.

DID YOU  KNOW?

The ironically named Treasure Island in San Francisco Bay was scraped together when millions of cubic yards of mud were pumped up from the bottom of the bay to create an island for the 1939 Golden Gate International Exposition. The event was "an extravaganza of culture and kitsch." The island is still there.

Extending an Olive Leaf...of LSD

An August 1965 anti-Vietnam War demonstration in Berkeley drew the wrath of the hawkish Hell's Angels motorcycle gang. The "Angels" ripped down banners and attacked protestors, yelling, "Go back to Russia, you f***ing communists!"

When the next peace demonstration approached, co-organizers Allen Ginsberg, Ken Kesey and other "Merry Pranksters" paid Angels' president Sonny Barger a visit at his home and discussed the situation over a few hits of LSD. The group reported that by dawn, everyone was happily chanting together. While the Hell's Angels remained pro-war, the group no longer disrupted peace demonstrations.

Unseemly Behavior

In May 1966, a California State Senate subcommittee released its 153-page assessment of conditions on the UC Berkeley campus. Calling the student activism "left-wing domination of the Berkeley campus," the report portrayed the school as a "montage of obscene entertainment, marijuana smoking, homosexuality and plotting, much of it by non-students, against the war in Vietnam." Yes, and the problem was...?

DID YOU KNOW?

In March 1966, California attorney general Thomas Lynch condemned the use of LSD and other recreational drugs. In October, the state legislature outlawed the sale and possession of LSD. Ah, come on, guys, lighten up!

The Naked Guy

A handsome young fellow named Andrew Martinez left his Cupertino home to attend school at UC Berkeley in 1990. By the time he arrived on campus, Martinez was already a dedicated nudist. At age 17, Martinez was inspired by the philosophy of Henry David Thoreau (who, as far as I know, kept his clothes on) to shed his clothing and go door to door asking neighbors if they minded.

While at UC, Martinez garnered national fame for his habit of attending parties and classes alike nude. He was photographed by *Playgirl* magazine and appeared on national TV talk shows. Apparently not everyone appreciated seeing his wanger, because in 1992, the university passed a dress code basically requiring students to wear *something*, and Martinez was expelled for refusing to comply.

DID YOU  KNOW?

Fortuna Rodeo organizers still talk about the year (they don't say which year) when the rodeo "went long hair" because Frederick Jagel of the Metropolitan Grand Opera Company sang there.

The Exotic Erotic Ball

Started in 1980 by Perry Mann and his partner Louis Abolafia, this San Francisco event has evolved from a nudist love fest (Abolafia claimed to have coined the phrase "Make Love, Not War") into a wild Mardi Gras–like party with participants and performers alike wearing scant lingerie, if anything at all. Groping will get you thrown out but, if you first get the gropee's permission, then it's called "fondling" and you can stay.

Medical Marijuana

In 1996, California voters approved the growth and use of marijuana for medical treatment with the passage of Proposition 215. Current estimates of the number of people using cannabis for medical reasons in California range from 150,000 to 350,000.

Many in the medical profession would like to be able to measure the results of this test case, but both those who prescribe and those who use the marijuana fear arrest if the political climate shifts, so few records are being kept. Dr. Tod Mikuriya founded the Society of Cannabis Clinicians (SCC) in an attempt to remedy the problem. The SCC collects confidential records that physicians can share to improve their use of medical marijuana.

Smoking

The number of smokers in California has dropped from 26 percent of the state's population in 1986 to 14 percent in 2005. Those who analyze these things say that the decline in smoking was caused by tobacco tax hikes. Proposition 99 of 1988 slapped a 25-cent-per-pack tax on cigs, with monies going to tobacco-use prevention and other health programs. Then in 1998, Proposition 10 added 50 cents per pack. In 2006, Proposition 86 proposed to up the smoking "sin tax" again, effectively raising the cost of the nicotine habit from $4 a pack to about $6.60. Ouch. Voters turned that one down.

Smokin' in the Boys Room

High school students in California cut back on smoking in even larger numbers than adults did…er, for a while. From 2000 to 2004, the numbers of high school smokers decreased from about 22 percent to about 13 percent. Then in 2006, 15 percent of high schoolers reported lighting up regularly. What happened, guys? Who knows, maybe they're just being more honest.

Go Ask Alice

Drug use in California seems to be creeping upwards among adults and teenagers alike, according to the National Surveys on Drug Use and Health.

In 2003, in a poll of a random group of adolescents between 12 and 17 years, 11 percent admitted to using illicit drugs in the last 30 days. Of those polled in 2004, 12 percent said they had recently tried the illegal stuff.

In a poll of adults—those 18 to 25 years old—in 2003, 18.8 percent said they had used illicit drugs in the last month. The next year, that number rose to 19.6 percent. Of the staid old fogeys 26 years and older, only about six percent, in both 2003 and 2004, admitted to illicit drug use.

EARLY CROSS-DRESSERS

Little Drummer Girl

Anna Hunley Glud lived out her adult years as a woman in Oakland, but she started her life as a boy, namely as the 10-year-old Civil War drummer boy called Tom Hunley. When General Grant laid eyes on the little ragamuffin, he tried to have him/her dismissed as too small to serve, but Glud's father intervened. At that point, the father admitted privately to Grant that "Tom" was a girl but explained to the General that the child was motherless, and he couldn't bear to leave her at home. Grant agreed to keep the little drummer in the force and swore himself to secrecy. "Tom" served the Union forces for two years.

Charlie Parkhurst

Back in the 1850s, stagecoach driver, or "whip," Charlie Parkhurst drove a "six up" (six-horse coach) with the best of them. Charlie was missing an eye from a horse's kick, kept a wad of tobacco stowed in one cheek, swore a blue streak and was a mean shot with a shotgun. Charlie was just like all the other stage drivers, except that when she got pregnant, she had to spend time out of sight to keep her secret...well, secrets. (Sadly, the baby died.)

Parkhurst outwardly lived her life as a man. She drove for the California Stage Lines until 1855 and then settled in Santa Cruz, where she drove the treacherous San José–Santa Cruz stage run. When she died in 1879, local papers broadcast the "shocking" secret of Charlotte "Charlie" Parkhurst.

DID YOU KNOW?

When Oscar Wilde performed in San Francisco in 1889, he said, "When people disappear they always seem to turn up in San Francisco." Now what could he have meant by that?

GAYS AND LESBIANS

Hot and Literary

Elsa Gidlow of San Francisco published her *On a Grey Thread*, the nation's first book of explicitly lesbian poetry, in 1923.

Howl

Beat poet Allen Ginsberg read his stream-of-consciousness poem "Howl" in public for the first time at the Six Gallery in San Francisco in 1955. "Howl" dealt openly with Ginsberg's homosexuality and with sexuality in general. When Lawrence Ferlinghetti, owner of City Lights Books, published *Howl and Other Poems* in 1957, police arrested the publisher on obscenity charges. The high-profile trial ended up as landmark anti-censorship legislation.

Daughters of Bilitis

The first known organization for lesbians was formed in San Francisco in 1955. The Daughters of Bilitis (DOB) took their name from French author Pierre Louv's book *Song of Bilitis*, which contained love poems between women. The DOB promoted civil rights for lesbians and provided a place for lesbians to socialize. The group published *The Ladder*, a national newsletter for lesbians, and held its first national convention in San Francisco in 1960.

Castro Street Fair

Along with the Pride March, one ebullient expression of Northern California's gay community happens every year at the Castro Street Fair, complete with drag queens and pep squads. The city's first openly gay city supervisor, Harvey Milk, started the fair in 1974, and it has become the city's longest-running street fair.

According to the 2000 U.S. Census, there are nearly 900 same-sex couples living together (each couple in their own home, presumably) in San Francisco.

San Francisco Dyke March

In June, the dyke community—some 50,000 strong—celebrates with a San Francisco march that starts in the city's Delores Park. The rules for the march are firm, including "Do not rev your bikes before the ride begins" and "No stunt riding," which includes wheelies, gals.

A group of San Francisco dykes, not on bikes but over dinner, organized the first dyke march in the country, which was held in Washington, DC, in 1993.

Tying the Knot the Same-Sex Way

On Thursday, February 12, 2004, newly elected mayor of San Francisco Gavin Newsom burst into the national spotlight by announcing that the City and County of San Francisco would be the first government body to issue marriage licenses to same-sex couples. More than 2700 gay and lesbian couples lined up outside City Hall the first week following Newsom's announcement and were wed. In August 2004, the Supreme Court called a halt to the marriages, saying that Newsom had overstepped his authority.

Contradictory Polls?

The only area in the state of California where voters approved of San Francisco Mayor Gavin Newsom's 2004 order to grant same-sex marriage licenses was the nine-county region surrounding San Francisco Bay. Voters there were in favor by 55 to 39 percent. In the polls that were conducted in the wake of the mayor's decision, 55 percent of the rest of the state's voters said they disapproved of same-sex marriages.

Polls sometimes can be contradictory. As opposed to the above results, when the same polling company asked voters during the same period if they supported President George W. Bush's proposed U.S. Constitutional amendment to make same-sex unions illegal nationwide, only 41 percent of Californians said they supported the amendment.

DID YOU KNOW?

Daughters of Bilitis founders Del Martin, 83 years old, and Phyllis Lyon, 80, were the first same-sex couple to marry at the San Francisco City Hall in February 12, 2004. At the time, Martin and Lyon had been together for more than 50 years.

WORK AND TAXES

That Gross Product

California's gross state product (GSP) was over $1.6 trillion in 2006, making it the largest in the country, according to the U.S. Department of Commerce.

The Nation of California

California's economy is currently the eighth largest in the world. If we pretend the state is actually a separate country (which neighboring states often wish it was, so they could keep some of the immigrants out, but I digress), it had a larger gross production in 2006 than all but seven nations in the world, outdoing even Canada and Spain.

DID YOU KNOW?

The U.S. state with the second largest economy in 2006 after California's—Texas—has a gross state product only 60 percent of California's.

Exports

The state exported $117 billion worth of goods in 2005, and all indications are that the number will continue to rise. The major markets were Asia, with the largest share at $52 billion, Europe, Mexico and Canada, one of the smaller of the big markets at $13 billion for the year.

Computer products were by far the largest export product, bringing $42 billion into the state in 2005. Agriculture was a distant fourth with $11 billion for the year.

Bringing Home the Bacon

The median annual income for a Californian household, as of 2005, was around $51,000. This places the state at 12th in the country. This sounds fine until you consider the mortgage on that fixer-upper you bought for half a million. (New Jerseyites take the cake in the paycheck department with a median household income of over $60,000 a year.)

Who We Work For

Most workers in California are employed in trades, transportation and the utilities sector. This is how the government (which measures these numbers) classifies jobs in retail, warehousing, import-export and transportation. In plain English, I think we're talking Target clerks and bus drivers here.

Three sectors come in a close second in terms of numbers of workers employed: the government (yes, all those lively souls in the post office and DMV), health and education (it's not clear why surgeons and kindergarten teachers get lumped into the same sector, but never mind), and professional and business services.

More Jobs?

Over the past 10 years, California has added 2.4 million jobs, a growth rate of 1.8 percent per year.

Pick up a Hammer and a Nail

While the bulk of the new jobs are in diverse sectors such as retail, transportation and government, the fastest growing sector has been construction, hammering away at an increase of 5.3 percent per year.

 DID YOU KNOW?

In order to save money, the state used convict laborers to build its roads into the 1970s.

Unemployment

California's recent unemployment rate—hovering between 4.5 to 5 percent—is close to the national average. The U.S. unemployment rate for 2005 was 5.1 percent.

Pink Slips

Manufacturing employment in California declined in the last decade, dropping 160,000 jobs. This is attributed mostly to the 2001–02 crash in the high-tech sector.

California's State Sales Tax

California has a state income tax with a 9.3 percent maximum variable rate. The state collects about $40 billion this way each year.

The sales tax you will pay in a given region of the state varies, between 7.25 and 8.75 percent. Sales taxes bring around $28 billion into the state's coffers annually.

Property taxes, based on fair market value of real estate, bring in about $33 billion a year in California.

DID YOU KNOW?

California pays more to the federal system that it receives back in direct monetary benefits.

Prop 13

Long-time Californians know all about "Prop 13," as the 1978 state proposition was called. Some loved it; some hated it. Either way, its repercussions are still felt today. Prop 13 stemmed the tide of rising property taxes, making it easier for homeowners to afford to stay. But it cut revenues drastically for social services—schools, libraries and other agencies—that had formerly benefited from those tax revenues. In 1977, before Prop 13, property tax revenues had come in at $10.3 billion. In 1979, after Prop 13, revenues were nearly halved to $5.7 billion.

The Burden We Bear

On average, a Californian pays a total of $10.96 per year for every $100 of personal income to cover all state and local taxes (not including what we put in Uncle Sam's outstretched hand). The national average is slightly less—at $10.74. Californians' tax burden falls in the range of that of other industrial states. Ohioans, for example, pay nearly $12 per $100 income, and New Yorkers shell out an average of $14 each.

What Are We Paying For Again?

California state and local taxes fund a long list of projects (such as school buildings) and services, including the following:

- ☛ K–12 education
- ☛ Assistance to low-income residents in need
- ☛ CalWORKs
- ☛ General assistance
- ☛ Child welfare
- ☛ Mental health services
- ☛ Substance abuse treatment
- ☛ Law enforcement and jails
- ☛ Trial courts
- ☛ Parks and recreational services
- ☛ Road maintenance

TRANSPORTATION

Lots o' Highways

Today California has about 50,500 miles of highway and free-way lanes. Local roads constitute another 327,000 miles.

Cars on Call

Californians have the reputation of being infatuated with their cars. However, numbers show that, on average, a Californian drives slightly fewer miles per year than do other Americans. On the other hand, we have more cars per person (not me, personally, but the collective "we") than our average countryman. It makes me wonder, do Californians spread their miles around among their "stable" of cars? Pretty sneaky.

DID YOU KNOW?

In Northern California, as in the rest of the country, even-numbered highways travel east–west and odd-numbered ones head north–south.

Northern California's Major Highways

Interstate 5 runs from Oregon in the north through the flat Central Valley and all the way into Mexico in the south. California State Route 99 was a U.S. highway until it was demoted in 1968 and I-5 took over that honor. Hurt and petulant, 99 sulks to this day on its way through agricultural hotspots such as Fresno and Modesto down to the Tehachapi Mountains inland of Santa Barbara.

Like I-5, U.S. Highway 101 also comes in from Oregon but takes a more coastal route southwards until, intimidated by the sheer number of freeways in L.A., it peters out altogether there.

As if the California highway system wasn't confusing enough, State Route 1, commonly called Highway 1, has an array of other official names, including "Cabrillo Highway" (south of San Francisco) and "Shoreline Highway" (north from Marin County). No matter what it's called, the route starts south of Eureka and twists its way (definitely not for the faint of stomach) to the southern edge of L.A. Highway 1 offers some of the most spectacular ocean views you'll ever see.

If you got on Interstate 80 in San Francisco and just kept driving, you'd eventually pull up in Teaneck, New Jersey, just outside the Big Apple. Inside California, I-80 travels through the state capital and across the Sierra Nevadas just north of Lake Tahoe into Reno on the Nevada side.

The Cost?

All state transportation needs in California cost $6.6 billion in the 2005–06 fiscal year. While public officials may talk a good line about public transit, the lion's share of the tax monies—nearly three-quarters of them—go to building and maintaining highways.

DID YOU KNOW?

Highway 101 is not only a road, it's a country-rock band, but don't let that confuse you.

By Land or By Sea

Northern California's Port of Oakland, though handling less material than Los Angeles, is one of America's predominant shipping ports. Container traffic through Oakland continues to rise, increasing by 47 percent in the last 10 years. The Port of San Francisco by comparison handles mainly non-containerized goods—such as lumber, cement and cars—and has nowhere close to Oakland's traffic.

Steamboat Service

The first regular steamboat service into California started in 1849 when the aptly (if less than imaginatively) named steamer *California*, run by the Pacific Mail Company, pulled into San Francisco Bay.

Sacramento became a major seaport in 1963, never mind the fact that it lies about 90 miles from the nearest shoreline. That's the year the capital city's deep-water channel was completed.

Riding the Rails

Much of the transcontinental railroad, which joined the Central Pacific Railroad out of Sacramento with Union Pacific from Omaha, was built by Chinese immigrants. The system was completed in 1869 and represented a big step forward for California transportation.

High Speed Wagons

The state's first highway was the Lake Tahoe Wagon Toll Road, which cut through the Sierra Nevada mountains from Sacramento to Nevada, by way of Lake Tahoe. The route, which today is known as Highway 50, doesn't get much wagon traffic anymore. It's just tough to get that ox team zero to 60 miles per hour in time to merge.

Mud Pies

One big motivation for the state of California to improve its roads and highways system was to improve agricultural commerce by helping get crops to markets. In the 1930s, the U.S. Bureau of Public Roads used the slogan "Get the farmer out of the mud" in its effort to improve rural roads.

First All-Weather Route Through the Sierras

When Squaw Valley won its bid for the 1960 Winter Olympics, it added impetus to a move to build an all-weather route through the Sierra Nevadas. Interstate 80, a divided highway, roughly parallels the route of the transcontinental railroad (completed in 1869) and passes close by the spot where the Donner party met its ill fate.

ENTREPRENEURS AND THEIR COMPANIES

First Millionaire

Sam Brannan became San Francisco's first millionaire in the 1850s by selling shovels and shirts to the gold miners.

What Brings in the Bucks?

What do you think of when you think of California products? Wine, perhaps, and almonds, along with computers and, of course, surfers. The area that makes the most money, it turns out, is financial services. Next are trade, transportation and utilities. Not all that sexy, guys. We need to find a way to increase the GSP (gross state product) of surfing.

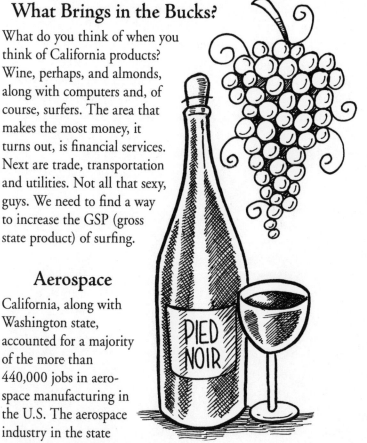

Aerospace

California, along with Washington state, accounted for a majority of the more than 440,000 jobs in aerospace manufacturing in the U.S. The aerospace industry in the state employed an average of 38,000 people in the last five years.

Who would have guessed that a plastic plate could be a toy company's cash cow? In 1977, Frisbees generated fully half of the Wham-O company's profits for that year. Fred Morrison, who received royalties for the design, told the *Los Angeles Times* that he had raked in $1 million by then.

Apple Computer

The first Apple computer—a clunky, ugly thing—debuted at a meeting of the Homebrew Computer Club in Palo Alto in 1976. At that time, no one even thought of calling the area Silicon Valley. Three computer geeks, Steve Jobs, Steve Wozniak, and Ronald G. Wayne, had formed the company on April Fool's Day of that year. Before founding Apple, Jobs and Wozniak reportedly split a monthly salary of $250. The next year, the founders moved the company out of Jobs' garage into a building in Cupertino. And, as they say, the rest...

COST OF LIVING

Sky-High Housing Prices

Anyone who has glanced at the classified ads (that would be Craigslist these days) knows that the cost of housing in sunny California is almost a joke. It would be hilarious except that those of us who live here have to pay the prices. How anyone (myself included) affords it remains a mystery.

The statewide median home price, as of mid-2006, was at an all-time high of $576,000. San Francisco tops the list of impossible places to buy unless your surname is Trump or Gates, with a median price of nearly $750,000. Median, mind you. (Orange County shares the honor.) The most affordable homes in California are found in the Central Valley, where you can pick up a gem for a mere $350,000.

Affording a Home

Housing prices reinforce and exacerbate the divide between the haves and the have-nots in Northern California. Even in the Central Valley, which has the most affordable homes, a person needs an annual income of over $67,000 to qualify for the average home loan. The Bay Area has the largest Homebuyer Income Gap Index in the state, according to the California Association of Realtors. There you need to pull in $151,340 (in 2004) to qualify for a median-priced home. Those of us who can't even imagine earning that much a year make up the rental market.

Country Mouse–City Mouse Income

In Northern California, the poverty rate is slightly higher in the city than in the country—13.2 percent of the city population falls below the poverty line versus 12.9 percent of country residents. While fewer rural residents live in poverty, however, their average income is lower than that of urban dwellers. In 2004, the average rural dweller earned $26,734, while the average city dweller earned $35,420.

Wage Gap

The minimum wage in California as of January 2007 was $7.50 per hour. If a minimum-wage employee works 40 hours per week all year, she (or he) earns $15,600 per year before taxes.

Meanwhile, in 2005, members of the state's top 10 percent highest-paid workers earned more than five times what each of the lowest-paid workers earned. For example, in the Northern California cities of Cupertino, San Ramon, Palo Alto and Pleasanton—each making *Money* magazine's "Biggest Earners in the U.S." list—the median household income is over $100,000.

AGRICULTURE

A Lot of Fruits and Nuts

The old (really really old, worn out, in fact) joke goes:

Why are Northern Californians like granola?

Because if you take away the fruits and nuts, all you have left are the flakes.

Ha, ha. Might as well get that out of the way. In an attempt to regain Californians' pride, however, I would like to point out that there are a lot of fruits and nuts in the state…along with dairy products, vegetables and fine wines.

Agriculture remains one of the state's predominant industries, just as it has been for the last 150 years. In fact, California is the fifth largest agricultural producer in the world. It has led the pack, as the number one agricultural producing and exporting U.S. state, for 50 years. So there.

Ripe Olive Mama

In 1895, at the age of 56, a Northern California woman named Freda Ehmann found herself widowed in Oroville without much money. What she did own was a 20-acre olive orchard at a time when olive oil prices had plummeted. Fat lot of good that would do her. Freda set to work anyway. She experimented with 280-gallon barrels of olives on her back porch, then she traveled north to British Columbia and to the east coast of the U.S., where she secured contracts for 10,000 gallons of olives when her orchard had only ever produced 1000 gallons. Somehow or other, this determined German immigrant pulled it off, launching a multimillion-dollar olive industry. In the process, Freda was dubbed the "Mother of the California Olive Industry."

Today, about 1200 growers produce up to 160,000 tons of olives a year in the warm Northern California valleys, primarily in Tulare, Glenn, Tehama and Butte Counties. The town of Oroville salutes Freda Ehmann.

Now That's Go-o-od Coffee

If you had walked into a store in Northern California (or just about anywhere in the nation) in the 1850s and asked for coffee, you would have gotten a handful of green beans. Around the time of the Gold Rush, anyone who drank coffee roasted and ground his or her own beans at home. When a 15-year-old named James A. Folger showed up in San Francisco in the fall of 1849, he had no idea that he would change all that. Folger, like every other hothead, hoped to get rich in the gold mines, but he had to work off his passage first. One thing led to another, and the young Folger worked for and ended up buying out the Pioneer Steam Coffee and Spice Mills in San Francisco, the first company in the West to sell roasted, ground coffee.

The State's Breadbasket

Northern California counties account for eight of the 10 top agricultural producers in the state, with SoCal's San Diego and Ventura counties coming in a lackluster eighth and ninth. (Okay, they've got Hollywood down there. Big whoop. We've got the cows.) Fresno County beats all others in the whole dang nation with $4.69 billion in agricultural income for 2004. All that sunshine makes for sweet grapes—Fresno's biggest commodity, which brought in $600 million in 2004.

Water, Water

California's rich agriculture is made possible, in large part, by the irrigation provided by the Central Valley Project. Constructed in 1937, the project consists of three dams, five canals and two power-transmission lines. The dams plug up numerous rivers, including the Sacramento, McCloud and Pit Rivers.

Horticulturist Luther Burbank

You can't talk about California's agriculture without mentioning this fellow. Coming out from Massachusetts, Luther Burbank settled in Santa Rosa in 1875. He developed some 800 new varieties of plants that revolutionized agriculture in the state. Rumor has it that Burbank developed the sharp-thorned blackberry bushes that are the bane of the backyard gardener. Supposedly Burbank saw the bushes as a way to provide free fruit to the masses.

DID YOU KNOW?

I heard it through the grapevine: the California raisin industry was started by accident in 1875 when Frances Eisen, known as the "Father of the Fresno Wine Industry," let some of his grapes dry on the vine.

Wine

Agoston Haraszthy was the first person in recorded history to have the idea, "Hey, let's grow wine in northern California so we can have tasting rooms that people will flock to and where they will buy lots of little wine-related gift items." Well, he didn't get that far, but the Hungarian immigrant did start vineyards in the 1850s, including one near San Francisco and another in Crystal Springs. In Sonoma County, Agoston planted a vineyard in which he experimented with new ideas such as storing wine in tunnels, using redwood for barrels and planting on hillsides.

OTHER INDUSTRIES

Black Gold

Remember the Beverly Hillbillies? Well, Jeb might have made his millions from oil before moving to California, but many Californians have made their fortunes that way without leaving home. In the early 1900s, major oil deposits were discovered in the San Joaquin Valley, Santa Barbara County and in the L.A. basin. (In the Roaring '20s, even more oil bubbled up throughout Southern California. L.A., at one time, was the largest oil-exporting port in the world.)

Mining

The Gold Rush gave California a kick-start, in terms of European development, back in 1848, when it drew tens of thousands of fortune hunters almost overnight. Today, gold is still mined in the state, though other minerals will make you richer these days.

As of 2004, California topped all the states in the amount of money made on mineral production (other than oil). In fact, minerals brought in $3.76 billion that year. What are mining companies digging up these days? Well, here's the list, in order of money made on each:

- construction sand and gravel
- Portland cement
- boron
- crushed stone
- gold
- clays
- gemstones
- silver

The Borax Magnates

While other guys were mining gold and going broke in the process, a fellow named William T. Coleman had the bright idea to mine "cottonball" from Death Valley. Cottonball is ulexite, which (in case that doesn't clear things up for you) is a compound used to make borax. Borax had been used for centuries in ceramics and goldsmithing, but it had always been imported from Tibet or Italy.

The story goes that a local doctor was testing the water in Death Valley for its medicinal properties and detected ulexite. Coleman filed claims on hundreds of acres of the glistening ore and set up Harmony Borax Works near what is now Furnace (get it—it's not that nice a place) Creek Ranch in Death Valley. Only trouble was, with no railroad anywhere nearby, how on earth do you transport thousands of pounds of ore?

The borax needed to go 165 miles across desert sand and over the Panamint Mountains, a 20-day trip by foot that led from 190 feet below sea level to 2000 feet above it. You've probably guessed by now, but I'll tell you anyway. The company used massive oak and steel wagons hauled by teams of 20 mules each. When the mules were all hitched in pairs, the team stretched out for 100 feet. Take it with a grain of borax, but the company swears that they didn't lose a single animal while using these 20-mule teams.

Coleman's fellow borax-a-tier, Francis Marion Smith, made his fortune off the stuff in Nevada before moving to the Bay Area to put his feet up. Actually, Mr. Smith kept busy. He built the Key System, a cutting-edge electric train that took East Bay commuters into San Francisco; he introduced speedy propeller-driven ferries to compete with the paddle-wheel crafts in use at the time; and he had the posh Claremont Hotel built in 1915. All that and borax, too!

Something's Fishy Here

The fishing industry in California is one of the top five in the country. Off the coasts of Northern and Central California, fishers harvest salmon, pink shrimp, swordfish, lobster, crabs and sole, to name just a few varieties.

Can you guess what the most lucrative critter to fish was during the 1990s? Sea urchins. They're delicious, if you can get around the spikes. No, seriously, sea urchins brought in about $20 million for the California fishing trade in the last decade.

Timber

California has long been a source of wood products for the nation and the world. But as supplies of forests have dwindled, so have the profits of the industry. In 1995, the total timber harvest was valued at $945 million, down 14 percent from the previous year. Oddly enough, though lumber mills have closed as production slows, employment numbers in the industry remain steady—providing an estimated 91,000 jobs in 1996.

California trees harvested for their wood include alder, Pacific maple, black oak, madrone, tan oak, myrtlewood (or pepperwood), claro walnut, yew, western red cedar and, of course, the beautiful and long-lasting redwood.

Environmental concerns—such as preservation of the endangered spotted owl—have come into conflict with traditional logging methods. Conflicts continue to rage over use of the state's remaining forestlands.

GENERAL HEALTH AND WELLNESS

Laid-Back Lives Longer

As a Californian, you can expect to live 80 years on average. This is longer than the national average of 78 (okay, not by much) and longer than what Californians' life expectancy was last year, so things just keep getting better. In fact, life expectancies have been steadily rising in the state since the 1950s. Maybe the stories about laid-back Californians have some truth to them.

Women, by the way, had an expected life span of 82 years to a man's 77. Pardon me if I say, "Nah, nah, nah, nah, nah."

Look Out! Here Come the Geriatric Boomers.

They're not babies anymore, folks. The population bump known as the Baby Boomers is moving into its golden years, in the Golden State as elsewhere. As the Boomers enter their 50s, they are pulling the state's average age up. The number of Californians over 65 years of age is predicted to increase almost three percent annually from 2006 to 2012. Compare that to a measly 0.5 percent increase for those 25 to 44 years old. (Are those the Gen-Xers? Sorry, shoved aside again, guys.)

California's Report Card on Health

The state's department of health has set itself some goals in terms of public health. It's proud to report that Californians are getting good grades—in most areas. Okay, okay, so rates of diabetes are on the rise as are drug use numbers. You can't have everything. The good news is that in recent years, California has reduced its teen birth rate, increased the percentage of mothers who breastfeed and lowered the death rate from almost all causes, including lung and breast cancer.

Havin' My Baby

California's fertility rate—at 70.4 births per 1000 women per year—is higher than the national average of 66.3 births. In 2004, that added up to 545,071 new bundles of joy.

Babies are Good…as Long as Mom is a Grown-Up

One of the state's public health goals is to reduce the number of teen pregnancies. Things are looking good in this department. Births to mothers between the ages of 15 and 19 years were down in the 2002–04 period. The most recent recorded rate of 39 births per 1000 teenage girls represents a 15-percent drop from rates three years ago.

Across the country teen births have also been declining. The national rate—only 20 births per 1000 teenage girls per year—is significantly lower than that in California.

Straight from the Source

Californian new mothers have increasingly chosen to breastfeed their babies, which everyone in the health field agrees is a good thing. Recent polls found that almost 84 percent of babes in the state eschewed the bottle, up from 82 percent a few years ago.

Health Costs Increasing

Californians spent less per person on health care in recent years than the national average. Personal health costs averaged $3429 per capita in California for 1998, as compared to a U.S. average of $3759. Most of this money went to pay doctors and hospitals.

Since 1991, it has cost a person on average 3.5 percent more each year to pay for healthcare. While increased demands on our pocketbooks is never welcome, at least Californians' costs increased more slowly than the national average, which was 4.9 percent per year over the same period. Hospitalizations caused by injuries cost $80 billion nationwide. There are an estimated six million people in California who don't have any health insurance.

Keeping Employees Healthy

Employers report spending an estimated $10,000 to $12,000 each year per employee just to cover the cost of health insurance premiums (not including the amount a person might pay for deductibles, co-insurances and other expenses).

The Rate at Which We Kick the Bucket

There's really no nice way to talk about death rates. It's buying the farm, folks. But California death rates are lower than the national average, in some cases (unintentional injuries and lung cancer, for instance) as much as 20 percent lower.

The 2002–04 average death rate in California was 704 per 100,000 people. That's down about nine percent since they last checked in 1999–2001. Meanwhile, in other parts of the country, the average was 801 per 100,000 people—and that was a record low.

Infant Mortality

Health administrators use infant mortality figures to see how a population is doing overall in terms of quality of health care. In California, the most recent infant mortality numbers are five deaths per 1000 infants, lower than the national average of around seven.

Rates vary widely from county to county. In 2004, Mendocino County had the highest infant mortality rate at nine per 1000, while nearby Sonoma Count had the state's lowest rate with 2.5 per 1000 infants.

There is concern among the state's healthcare professionals because, unfortunately, the African-American infant mortality rate remains twice as high as the rate among whites.

Okay, So We Don't Drive So Well

Californians must be yakking too much on their cellphones while they drive. Between 2000 and 2003, the deaths from motor vehicle accidents each year shot up from about 3800 to 4300.

In spite of what they tell you, boys do drive worse than girls, or at least more recklessly. According to the California Department of Health Services, the motor vehicle accident death rate in 2003 for males was more than double that for females.

AIR QUALITY

Asthma is a Rising Concern

Doctors and public health professionals are concerned with recent indicators that the number of people suffering from asthma in California is on the rise. The percentage of youngsters aged one to 17 with asthma increased from 14 percent in 2001 to 16 percent in 2005. Adults showed a rise, over the same period, from 11 percent to almost 13 percent.

DID YOU  **KNOW?**

The salt marshes around San Francisco bred huge clouds of malaria-bearing mosquitoes in the early 1900s. There were so many that commuters waiting for the Marin to San Francisco ferry had to wear head nets.

Get a Gas Mask

Another one of the state's public health goals is to reduce the number of people exposed to too much ozone. (Does that mean smog?) Alas, California flunks this one in a big way. I guess if you're going down, you might as well go down big. The goal here is zero. So you'll see that all is not well when, in every county in California but one, 80 percent or more of residents are exposed to too much ozone.

The one place you can breathe easy in the state? Tulare County, north of Bakersfield, where only 32 percent of the people breathe unacceptable ozone levels.

Leaders in Clean Air Standards

For a long time, the city of Los Angeles brought to mind what? Hollywood, oranges and...smog. On September 8, 1943, when hundreds of Angelinos complained of stinging eyes, nausea and vomiting, it wasn't just a massive hangover. It was the first recognized episode of smog in the nation.

While L.A. cleaned up its act, the San Francisco Bay Area took proactive measures. The 1966 auto emission standards of the state's Motor Vehicle Pollution Control Board were the first of their kind in the country. In 1973, the Bay Area was one of the first districts in the world to adopt a gasoline vapor recovery program.

It's probably no coincidence that for 1996 through 1998, the Bay Area was one of the only urban areas to have acceptable ozone levels.

A WEIGHTY ISSUE

Diabetes and Obesity Are On the Rise

Like the rest of the country, California is experiencing an increase in diabetes. In 2005, seven percent of adults were diagnosed with the disease as compared to 6.6 percent in 2003.

Obesity is a risk factor for a number of diseases, including diabetes. In 2005, obesity increased in adults to 21 percent, up from 19 percent four years earlier.

Hubby is Chubbier (in California)

Put down that beer! Men in California are a bit more overweight than their female counterparts. In 2003, 21 percent of California's men were obese and 20 percent of its women. National numbers, however, give her the Couch Potato Prize, with 34 percent of women obese to just 30 percent of men.

Little Couch Spuds

The Couch Potato Prize has a junior version. Recent studies have found that nearly one in three California kids spend three hours or more each weekday in front of the TV. As for the teenagers, one quarter of all California teens reported that they had exercised less than 30 minutes—we're talking total, here—in

the last week. In fact, sad but true, only about one-quarter of all kids from fifth grade to ninth grade can meet the state's basic fitness standards.

NOTABLE PEOPLE AND EVENTS IN HEALTH

Recombinant DNA

Biochemist Herbert Boyer of UC San Francisco teamed up with medical professor Stanley Cohen of Stanford University to successfully invent the first recombinant DNA in 1972.

Boyer went on to co-found the groundbreaking biotech company Genentech. Cohen was awarded the 1986 Nobel Prize in Physiology.

Harnessing the Genetic Magic

Call it black magic or a medical miracle, the scientific revolution of the biotechnology industry began in the San Francisco Bay Area. On April 7, 1976, financier Bob Swanson and scientist Herbert Boyer teamed up to incorporate Genentech, Inc. The company set out to make use of breakthroughs in gene-splicing techniques to create new medicines. The resulting biotechnology industry has made dizzying advances in the last 25 years— changing the way medicines (and other industrial products) are conceived and produced.

In 1972, while Boyer was a researcher at the University of San Francisco, he had, along with Stanley Cohen of Stanford University, been the first to show that genes from one creature could be spliced into bacteria. The altered bacteria would then crank out the desired proteins.

In the ensuing years, Genentech has produced a number of famous products, including a piece of the insulin gene, a growth hormone to combat dwarfism in children, and—for agribusiness giant Monsanto—the controversial bovine growth hormone that increases milk production in dairy cattle.

The company has also derived products as diverse as industrial enzymes to remove grease from clothes and antibodies designed to target cancerous tumors.

DID YOU KNOW?

UC Berkeley professor of entomology Charles Woodworth was the first person to breed fruit flies intentionally. What sounds like a disgusting idea (don't you hate those things hovering over your compost bucket?) turned out to be a scientific break-through. Woodworth suggested that the troublesome little crit-ters, *Drosophila*, could be used to study genetics. Geneticists agreed and made full use Woodworth's little friends.

Eau D'Pope

Well, you'll all be delighted to know that California's doctors are keeping busy in their spare time. As an example, 69-year-old Dr. Fred Hass (incidentally, the brother of ex-U.S. Poet Laureate Robert Hass) claims to have re-created the cologne used by Pope Pius IX in the 19th century. The good doctor cooked the per-fume up in his San Rafael kitchen from a recipe he found in a limited-edition 1963 cookbook.

The doctor has brewed 2000 bottles worth of the smelly stuff, which he's storing in his garage for the time being, and has approached major depart-ment stores and perfume companies with his secret blend. His two-ounce bot-tles go for $24.99. He describes the scent as fresh with hints of citrus and violet.

Pope Pius IX served from 1846 to 1878. He was known for instituting papal infallibility and the Immaculate Conception as church dogma and for granting amnesty to political prisoners. I don't mean to be a spoilsport, but it's never been particularly high on my list to smell like a pope, even one famed for his humanitarian policies.

California's First Doctor, Sort Of

John Marsh, the first recorded doctor in California, practiced with a bachelor's degree he passed off as an MD because the local authorities couldn't decipher the Latin on the diploma.

It was from Harvard, after all—that was pretty impressive—and he had studied with a couple of doctors.

Traveling out from the eastern U.S., Marsh bought 17,000 acres in the shadow of Mt. Diablo in 1837 to fulfill his dream of being a rancher. With the help of local Native Americans, he built a small adobe house there. When not tending to his land, Marsh tended to the medical needs of citizens from his adobe hospital. The rancher and doctor idea worked especially well, because Marsh took payment in cattle, as well as in furs and tallow. His practice eventually beefed up (sorry, I couldn't resist) his herd to nearly 6000 head.

Fiddletown's Famous Doctor

The lure of gold tempted fortune hunters from around the globe, including, in 1850, a 25-year-old man from Toisan, China. Yee Fung Cheung was from a distinguished family. Like his father, he was a trained herbal doctor, but that didn't prevent him from succumbing to gold fever.

Yee Fung Cheung settled in a town called Fiddletown, which boasted the largest Chinese population in California outside of San Francisco. The young man quickly found that he prospered better as a doctor in Fiddletown than he did as a miner, partly because of laws that discriminated against Chinese miners. He established a medical practice in a rammed-earthen adobe store, where he treated his fellow Chinese miners and later many of the Chinese laborers who built the transcontinental railroad.

Yee Fung Cheung became famous among white Californians when he saved the life of Governor Leland Stanford's wife. Western doctors had given up on Mrs. Stanford's severe lung disease, when the family's Chinese cook sought out Yee Fung Cheung, whom he found playing a game of mahjong at the Wah Hing Grocery in Sacramento. The Chinese doctor treated the invalid with herbs, including "majaung," and Mrs. Stanford recovered. Western medicine later discovered majaung to be a natural source of ephedrine, a medicine now widely used to treat pulmonary problems.

Yee Fung Cheung's story has an ironic side note. The governor and his staff called the doctor Wah Hing, after the grocery where they located him. After he saved Mrs. Stanford's life, Yee Fung Cheung was ever after known to the (can you say "clueless"?) non-Chinese people as Dr. Wah Hing. Hey, has anyone seen Dr. Safeway around?

Yee Fung Cheung retired and returned to China in 1904, where he died three years later. His descendents stayed in the Sacramento area, and many of them continue the family's healing tradition today as dentists and physicians. Yee Fung Cheung's original adobe herb store, the Chew Kee Store, has been fully restored by Fiddletown and is listed in the National Register of Historic Places.

The First Medical School on the West Coast

Dr. Elias Cooper and his nephew Dr. Levi Cooper Lane joined forces to open the first medical school on the West Coast in 1859. Located in San Francisco, the school was named Medical Department of the College of the Pacific. Six physicians taught 13 students. The school graduated a total of 28 students in its six-year life.

God's Hotel

In the early days of California's development, the railroads were king. Rail transit brought in people and supplies, and railroad company executives raked in fortunes and became prominent state citizens. It's not as weird as it might sound today, therefore, that the city of Sacramento was glowingly proud when the first railroad hospital in the world opened on its streets in 1870.

The four-story building was located on 13th and C streets. It could house 125 patients, all passengers or employees injured in railway accidents. In the early days, horse-drawn city vans brought patients who couldn't stand up. Horse-drawn "hotel buses" carried patients who were more able. From its opening until 1877, the hospital was proud to lose only 148 of the 3600 patients it treated. The French citizenry referred to the place, for all of its good works, as *Hôtel Dieu*, meaning "God's Hotel."

The railway hospital was moved to San Francisco in 1899, and the old hospital building, used for other purposes, was vacated in the 1970s and was torn down in 1986.

First County Hospital in Bakersfield

At the spot where Bakersfield High School now stands, early Kern County residents erected the first county hospital in 1875. The one-story cabin was made of redwood and cost $1400. Within two weeks, Dr. H.S. Bachman had four patients.

Unfortunately, the hospital was located on the edge of a swamp full of malaria-bearing mosquitoes. That was definitely bad for business, as was the allegedly haunted Reeder house across the street. The hospital was in use for 20 years, but the town's well-heeled citizens tended to seek medical attention elsewhere.

Bay Area biotech giant Genentech was accused of slipping into UC San Francisco's labs and stealing crucial genetic material that later enabled it to produce its break-out product—the sought-after human growth hormone.

Henry J. Kaiser: Founder of the HMO

Perhaps more than any other single person, Henry J. Kaiser influenced the history of California in the early 1900s. During World War II, Kaiser's shipyards launched more ships than any other builder. His company was the first to manufacture steel on the West Coast, and it completed the massive Hoover and Grand Coulee dam projects.

Inspired by a 12-bed field hospital set up in 1933 to serve aqueduct workers in the Mojave Desert, Kaiser developed a healthcare organization in Richmond to treat his wartime shipyard workers. It became the model for HMOs nationwide. Unlike many HMOs, however, Kaiser's system was and remains a not-for-profit organization. Today Kaiser Permanente is America's largest nonprofit health care organization, serving over eight million subscribers.

The Inspiring Dr. Lee

Fresno-born Sammy Lee was the child of Korean immigrant parents. His father dreamed that Sammy would become a doctor someday. For his part, the boy dreamed of becoming an Olympic athlete. Sammy faced hurdles in both pursuits, partly because of his ethnic heritage. For instance, Sammy could only swim on Wednesdays, the day the pool was open to non-whites.

Lee worked his way through the University of Southern California School of Medicine, receiving his MD in 1947. Just a year later, Dr. Lee made Olympic history, taking a gold medal for the 10-meter platform dive in the 1948 London Olympic games as the first Asian American ever to take gold at the Olympics. Four years later, he won gold again in the 10-meter and bronze in the three-meter springboard at Helsinki.

Dr. Lee went on to coach the U.S. Olympic Diving Team for the 1960 and '64 games. He was elected to the International Swimming Hall of Fame in 1968. In 1976, Lee coached diver Greg Louganis in his silver-medal Olympic performance.

TRENDS IN EDUCATION

Land of Many Languages

While a state's literacy rate indicates the level of education of its residents, interpretation of California's literacy rate is made more complex by the large number of citizens who speak a language other than English. If you don't speak or read English, it's tough to score well on standardized English tests.

☞ According to the U.S. Census, five million adults in California—that's about 22 percent—speak a language other than English at home.

☞ California ranked first in the nation in the number of students not fluent in English—25 percent in 2003–04. By comparison, the national figure is around eight percent.

☞ The most common language spoken, other than English, is Spanish. About 20 percent of California residents speak Spanish. A distant second is Chinese, followed by Tagalog and Vietnamese.

☞ In all, over 200 languages are spoken in the state.

The Official State Language

The question of whether or not to accommodate non-English speakers in California raises furor. Some believe strongly that those who move to California need to assimilate by learning English. Others believe that it's important to help new immigrants make the transition from a foreign language into English or not transition at all but keep their mother tongue. The question is pertinent in educating children of immigrants—should schools offer instruction in languages other than English?

In 1986, voters changed the state constitution to specify English as the official language of California. In practice, however, schools and other social services often offer some level of translation, especially into the second most commonly used language in California, Spanish.

Functionally Illiterate

There is another group that doesn't score well on standardized tests. An estimated two million native English speakers in California are functionally illiterate. These are people who cannot read, write or do math problems at a basic level.

DID YOU  KNOW?

The public school system in California is vast. It serves six million students in more than 9500 schools.

Education

Education numbers differ depending on whether a northern Californian lives in a city or the country. More rural residents complete high school—82 percent—than do their city counterparts—77 percent (in 2000). But more urban youngsters complete college—about 27 percent—than do rural residents—18 percent. This could reflect income differences (it's tough to pay for college on a lower income) or maybe it just shows that many rural job skills come from hands-on experience. In other words, you don't need a master's degree to drive a tractor.

Diversity

California schools are the most diverse in the nation in terms of ethnic and cultural heritage. The state's schools no longer have a majority ethnic group. In 2003–04, students identified themselves in the following groups: Hispanic/Latino (46 percent), white (33 percent), Asian (11 percent) and African American (8 percent).

By comparison, in the nation as a whole, the average classroom composition is 58 percent white, 19 percent Hispanic/Latino, 17 percent African American, four percent Asian and one percent Native American.

Enrollment Levels Off or Declines

Overall K–12 enrollment is expected to stop growing in California in the near future. The number of children in elementary school began to decline in 2004 and is expected to continue going down. High school enrollment is predicted to increase modestly for the next few years and then also decline.

Fluctuations in the number of students are expected to vary with each county. Large urban districts such as San Francisco are expected to decline by five percent or more in the near future, while some more rural counties—including San Joaquin, Kern and Sacramento—expect to see increases of as much as 26 percent. The most precipitous projected decline in northern California is for remote Modoc County, with a decrease of 20 percent.

Parents in San Francisco County send their kids to private school more than parents in any other county in California. Thirty percent of San Francisco children attend private school, as compared to only 19 percent in posh Marin and 11 percent in L.A.

Teachers Are Going Home

The retirement rate of California's teachers is on the rise and is expected to jump further. More and more K–12 teachers are choosing a lounge chair and a good show on cable TV over the scintillating experience of herding a bunch of eight-year-olds towards academic achievement. There appears to be yet another example of fallout from the baby boom: many active teachers will be arriving at retirement age within the next several years.

Hmm, let's see. If enrollment declines and teachers retire, perhaps schools will be phased out entirely soon.

Poverty Among Schoolchildren

In spite of its wealth and reputation as an affluent state, many of California's residents just barely scrape by. In 2003–04, almost half (48 percent) of the children in California schools came from low-income families. Nationally, the average is 37 percent. Low-income status was determined by whether or not a student was eligible for federal meal programs.

Achievement Depends on Income Status

Students from low-income families scored lower on state academic tests than did those from middle- and high-income families. Only 26 percent of low-income sixth graders, for example, scored as proficient or better on the tests, while 60 percent of better-off kids did.

Uh Oh, Spaghetti-O

Apparently it's high time for California educators and their students to hit the books. The state ranked in the bottom six states in the U.S. in every one of the most recent national performance tests. Half of its fourth-graders and 40 percent of its eighth-graders scored below the basic level in reading. Students did a little better in math, with 29 percent of fourth-graders and 43 percent of eighth-graders below the basic mark.

Of all the ethnic groups, the Latino students showed the greatest improvements in their scores between 2003 and 2005.

Hmm, Could There Be a Correlation?

California has an abysmal student-teacher ratio. With more than 20 students for every school employee, the state ranks nearly last in the entire nation, with only Arizona and Utah ranked worse. The ratio, educators say, does not represent true classroom size. Since it includes all school staff; classes are even bigger than 20 students.

Yikes! California ranked dead last in numbers of librarians and guidance counselors per student.

The Good News

On the bright side, the percentage of students having at least basic levels in reading and math has been increasing since 2002. In other words, test scores are improving.

Of course, plenty of teachers argue that standardized tests are a sorry way to measure a student's learning overall, but that's another book entirely.

The Cost of an Education

The standard way to measure a state's investment in its pupils is dollars spent per student. At $7584 per child in 2003–04, California ranks close to the national average for K–12 spending. This is an improvement over past years, when the state spent significantly below the national average.

Private Schools

Since the 2000–01 school year, enrollment in public schools has increased by four percent, while enrollment in private schools in California has decreased by eight percent. Nevertheless, nearly 600,000 California youngsters attend private school.

Sixty-three percent of private schools in the state are church-affiliated, with two-thirds of these Roman Catholic.

By far the majority of northern California's private schools are coeducational and day schools. None of that old New England *Dead Poets' Society* boarding school stuff for the Golden State.

OLDEST SCHOOLS

Oldest School in the State

A ramshackle old adobe near the Santa Clara Mission was apparently the first school opened for American children in California. In December 1846, a stalwart soul named Mrs. Olive M. Isbell got it underway. She reported that, lacking slates, the children wrote on their hands in order to learn their letters. Don't try that at home, kids.

First School in Sacramento, Briefly

The first school opened on the corner of Third and I streets in what is now the state capital in 1849. A month later, the school closed because of low enrollment.

Fresno has the two oldest school buses in service not only in northern California but in the entire state as of December 2006 when the Mojave Desert schools finally retired "School Bus One" from regular service to the occasional parade. So far, Fresno's San Joaquin Valley Unified School District keeps its 1959 models up and running. One odd thing about this topic is that the state sees fit to maintain a running (so to speak) list of the oldest school buses at all.

First Public School

A Yale graduate, Thomas Douglas was the teacher at the first American public school in San Francisco. The school opened its doors on April 3, 1848, a few months after gold was discovered at Sutter's Mill. When reports came soon after of the yellow stuff at Coloma, however, it was too much for the dedicated educators to resist. The trustees and Mr. Douglas alike grabbed their mining pans and headed for the hills.

Okay, Let's Try That Again

It wasn't until a year after the first attempt at a public school in San Francisco failed that a lasting one was established in northern California. In the fall of 1849, John and Amanda Pelton opened a school in San Francisco's old Baptist Church. It was initially free only to the poorer students, but the city council adopted an ordinance in 1850, making the education free to all.

The first city school system in the entire state was formed around Pelton's little public school. From this humble beginning sprouted the first budding layers of what is now a massive state education bureaucracy.

The First University

Northern California's University of California at Berkeley was the first of the state's now prestigious universities. It had a drawn-out founding, starting with nothing more than a hope expressed in the state's first constitutional convention in 1849 for a state university. In 1853, a group of clergy hoping to save souls among the gold miners opened Contra Costa Academy in Oakland, which they later renamed the College of California.

In 1866, the federal government deeded 150,000 acres for a college that would teach agriculture and mechanical arts. Thus the Agricultural, Mining and Mechanical Arts College was created, but without a campus to sit on. (It seems they sold the land.) The College of California merged with the new college into a larger institution and, in 1868, the first University of California was created from an odd conglomeration of religious and industrial ideals.

A year later, when the university doors opened, there were 10 faculty members and 40 students.

Oldest and Best Spin Artist

One trick to being oldest is to define your category so narrowly that no one else can argue with you. Here are just a few examples:

- San Francisco–based New College of California boasts the "oldest public-interest law school in the country."

- Chinese American International School in San Francisco is, according to the school itself, "the nation's pre-eminent and oldest independent school offering Chinese-English immersion education." Fair enough.

- UCSF School of Pharmacy, founded in 1872, was "the first pharmacy school in the West," a.k.a. the oldest. Given that the state was only founded 22 years before that, I think they might have a point there.

And probably my favorite qualification (because it's so useful):

- Northwestern California University, an online law school in Sacramento, is the "oldest law school *of its type* with continual operation in California." Emphasis mine. I'm considering adding to my résumé, "Most intelligent woman of her type in the world."

HIGHER LEARNING

The UC System

California has an unusual, three-tiered ladder of postsecondary education. Probably the most famous element is the University of California, with many world leaders on staff, including the largest number of Nobel laureates of any institution in the world.

What started in Berkley with 10 instructors and 40 students back in 1869 has expanded into a 10-campus operation, enrolling over 170,000 students. Including affiliated national laboratories and research stations across the state and overseas, the UC now employs over 41,000 faculty members and has an annual budget of over $11 billion.

Northern California UC campuses are located in Berkeley, Davis, San Francisco, Merced and Santa Cruz. There are also five Southern California campuses.

California State Universities

Intended mainly for undergraduates, the state universities are the middle tier on California's higher-education ladder. Their enrollment of over 400,000 students on 23 campuses makes it the largest university system in the country. The universities are also proud to claim the title of "the most diverse and one of the most affordable university systems in the country." In general, state universities admit the top third of graduating high school students.

California Community Colleges

Arguably the workhorses of California's postsecondary education are its community colleges. At 109 and counting, the colleges serve about three million students.

DID YOU KNOW?

In 1900, at a time when most other colleges either excluded or limited female enrollment, 60 percent of UC Berkeley's students were women.

Hey, Is That Fair?

The UC receives almost four times as much state funding per student as do the low-on-the-totem-pole community colleges, while the California state universities receive twice as much as the community colleges.

California has a unique state constitutional amendment requiring approximately 40 percent of state revenues to be spent on education.

Private Colleges

Northern California is home to some of the nation's finest private colleges and universities. Perhaps the first one that comes to mind for most people is Stanford University, located in Palo Alto. This part of the state also boasts such institutions as the San Francisco Art Institute and Mills College in Oakland.

Stanford: Almost Ivy League?

Stanford University, founded in 1891, is one of the country's most prestigious universities. In spite of its excellence, the university tends to have a bit of a little brother complex, as evidenced by popular t-shirts announcing first "Stanford: the Harvard of the West" and later, with more wit (but still seen on the Stanford campus): "Harvard, the Stanford of the East."

Complex notwithstanding, Stanford has many illustrious claims to fame, including 17 living Nobel laureates on staff and a starring role in creating the high-tech Silicon Valley region, with Stanford faculty or alumni helping start such household-name companies as Google, eBay and Hewlett Packard.

Well-Paid Profs

California pays its college and university professors the highest salaries in the nation. The average in 2004–05 was $100,000. Compare that with the national average of $70,000 and with the nation's lowest-paid educators in South Dakota, who receive $50,000 a year.

That sounds great, but before all of you academics whip out your résumés, consider the cost of living. The median home price in San Francisco teeters at a lofty $750,000, while you can bed down comfortably in South Dakota for $80,000.

DID YOU KNOW?

UC Berkeley today has the largest foreign student enrollment (4000) in the nation.

What a Deal!

Students in California's community college or state university systems pay by far the lowest student fees per unit of any other comparable institution in the country. UC students pay the second lowest fees in the nation. (This is true for in-state students only.)

In all of California's state colleges and universities, the student fees don't come close to paying the cost of the education received. A UC student's fees cover one-third of the cost; a state college student's cover one-quarter; and a community college student's only cover one-eighth. State taxpayers pick up the rest of the bill.

And the Bill Is...

In the 2005–06 school year, the state general fund doled out $2 billion for the UC, $2 billion for the state colleges, and $5.5 billion for the community colleges.

State Funding Doesn't Target Needy Students

If you were in charge of doling out scholarships, you might consider giving them to the students whose families had the least money. I would. But not the California state government. The state subsidizes all students. Funds targeted for low-income students only make up 12 percent of overall support in the UC system and only six percent in the state and community colleges.

Be Prepared

A whopping 55 percent of California state college students started college with less than basic proficiency in either reading or math in 2005. In fact, only 45 percent of incoming students were proficient in both areas at the get-go.

NOTABLE PEOPLE AND EVENTS

Mrs. Olive M. Isbell: Founder of the State's First School

A young woman trudged into Northern California in 1846, with a band of other immigrants who had just made a rough journey across the plains. Service-minded to the core, the woman, who soon married to become Mrs. Olive M. Isbell, opened a school in an old adobe building near the Santa Clara Mission. This was the state's first school for American children. Mrs. Isbell didn't rest on her laurels for long, however. A few months later, she opened a second school in an old customhouse in Monterey.

DID YOU KNOW?

When the California Constitution was drafted, members of the constitutional convention saw no reason to reinvent the wheel. They borrowed the provisions on education, almost word for word, from the Constitution of Michigan, which had been drafted 12 years earlier.

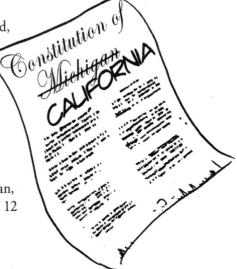

John Swett: Unsung Hero for Public Education

It took decades after the first American school opened in the state for California to get its public education system up and running smoothly. When the leaders weren't rushing off to the gold fields, they were fighting among themselves. A northern California man named John Swett, who became superintendent of public instruction in 1863, finally got things underway.

During his tenure, Swett made the schools free in all districts for at least part of the year, ensured that better schoolhouses were built, established school libraries, provided certification for teachers and made sure that teachers were adequately paid. That's naming just a few of Swett's achievements.

The First Teacher in Oakland

Hannah Jane Adams came out from New York state with her husband in the 1850s. He got busy developing the land around Lake Merritt; she opened Oakland's first school in 1855.

Jane Lathrop Stanford

Many people know that Stanford University was named after Leland Stanford Jr. Some know that the young man was the son of railroad magnate and Republican state governor Leland Stanford. A few know that the fellow died when only 15 years old from typhoid fever and that his tragic death inspired his brokenhearted parents to found the university. But did you know that, without the stewardship of Jane Lathrop Stanford, the young man's mother, the university, which is now one of the top in the nation, would probably have come to as premature an end as did its unfortunate namesake?

Leland Stanford Sr., the boy's father, died just two years after helping found the university in 1891. His death left his affairs in a state of chaos that threatened to sink the university, which depended on Stanford's funding for its existence. Jane Lathrop Stanford, though a grieving widow, stepped forward. She guided the university through its inception, even turning over her household money to ensure its survival. In 1903, with the school on sound footing, she passed leadership over to her handpicked board of trustees.

DIVISION OF POWER

The First Partiers

The country's two leading political parties started early on in California's statehood. A meeting was held on October 25, 1849, to organize the California Democratic Party. Just a few years later, railroad man Leland Stanford, along with Collis Huntington, Charles Crocker and Mark Hopkins—sometimes called the Big Four—put together the state's Republican Party in 1856.

It's the Democrats Out of the Gates... And the Republicans in the Stretch

Immediately following the drafting of California's constitution in 1850, the Democratic Party dominated the state's elections. The flamboyant Irish American David Broderick served as U.S. senator because of, or perhaps in spite of, his strong anti-slavery stance. When Broderick was killed in a duel, many Democrats switched to the state's nascent Republican Party and helped sweep Abraham Lincoln to presidential victory in 1860. With the 1861 election of Leland Stanford to the governorship, the state began two decades in Republican hands.

Early Mayhem

Chaos reigned in Gold Rush San Francisco. With no official police force, one group of thugs attacked another at will. The world's first millionaire, Sam Brannan, organized a vigilante committee. Unfortunately, the committee itself got out of control for a time. In 1956, it seized control of the city and tried and hanged anyone its members didn't like.

Railroads Were King

In the late 1800s, railroad companies and their executives, such as Governor Leland Stanford, held a lion's share of power in early California. While a worker on the rails earned about $2 a week, Stanford spent a million dollars in one year to build his mansion.

The Workingmen's Party

Huge discrepancies between the haves and have-nots in the 1870s spurred the Workingmen's Party to form in San Francisco in 1877. With the fiery speaker Denis Kearney at its head, the Party called for an eight-hour workday, restraints on the railroad's power and bank reform. Among other inflammatory remarks, Kearney said that, if the condition of workers was not improved, his party would see that "bullets would replace ballots."

The Progressive Party

By 1910, a statewide movement formed the Progressive Party and elected reform candidate Hiram Johnson as governor by a landslide. Johnson succeeded in weakening not just the power of the railroads but of the political parties. In a move to give more power to the voters, he created the proposition process that later led to such direct voter initiatives as Prop 13.

Japanese Americans

In 1905, San Francisco's Asiatic Exclusion League (headed by the city's labor leaders) convinced the city to segregate Japanese school children, along with other Asians. President Theodore Roosevelt persuaded the city to drop its segregation mandate but only when he promised and delivered in 1907 an agreement that forbade any more Japanese workers from entering the U.S. In 1942, after Japan bombed Pearl Harbor, thousands of Japanese-American Californians were herded into concentration camps.

DID YOU KNOW?

Ronald Reagan's tenure as California governor was flanked on either side by an Edmund G. Brown. He was preceded in the office by Edmund G. "Pat" Brown Sr. and succeeded by Edmund G. "Jerry" Brown.

An Increasing Number of Latino Voters

The share of registered voters who identify themselves as Latino has nearly doubled in the last 10 years, from 10 percent in 1990 to 19 percent in 2005. Latinos in California have traditionally voted two to one for Democrats.

DID YOU KNOW?

The first California-born California governor was Romualdo Pacheco, elected in 1875.

Absentee Voting

More and more voters from all parties are signing up to vote by mail, which has significantly raised voter turnout.

DID YOU KNOW?

Merced County, due east of San José, has a nearly perfect record in choosing the winning presidential candidate. As of 2004, Merced residents had voted for the winning candidate in 22 of the past 24 presidential elections. (No county had a perfect record.)

Voters of Color

Minority groups have a way to go in achieving equal representation at the polling booths. An estimated 1.2 million people of color are registered but don't vote, and another 3.7 million are eligible but haven't registered.

Northern Californians Get Out to Vote

While statewide voter turnout has been dismal, Northern Californians still flock (relatively) to the polls. In 2006, with only 30.5 percent of eligible voters getting off their fat sofas across the state, six northern counties turned out more than 50 percent—Alpine, Amador, Modoc, Sierra, Trinity and Tuolumne. In the 2005 election, all 10 of the counties that turned out more than 60 percent of its voters were also in northern California.

Republican Blues

The last year, a Republican candidate won either a presidential or senate election in the Golden State was in 1988. In his 2000 bid for the White House, George W. Bush sank $15 million in California—and still lost it. Prior to 1988, the conservative

Southern Cal stronghold had historically served as a springboard for Republican Party candidates such as Earl Warren and Ronald Reagan.

DID YOU KNOW?

California's electorate—at 17 million voters and counting—is the largest in the U.S.

The Decliners

In Santa Clara County, the home of Silicon Valley, voters who "Decline to State" their choice of political party may soon replace Republicans as the second biggest political "party." From 1996 to 2002, while the number of registered Democrats shrunk by two percent (to 46 percent) and the number of Republicans decreased by four percent (to 30 percent), the Decliners gained six points, to go from 13 percent to 19 percent.

Decliners tend to be women, younger, techies (not surprising in Silicon Valley) and, increasingly, of Asian heritage.

The Coastal/Inland Divide

California voters are diverging along urban-rural lines. Coasties tend to be college grads, more are unmarried, and they have higher incomes. More Inlanders are married, don't have college degrees, earn lower incomes and are born-again Christians. Coasties go Democratic by double digits, while the Inlanders go equally big for Republicans.

NOTABLE FIGURES

How I Ended Poverty

Former Socialist and well-known writer Upton Sinclair ran as a Democrat for California governor in 1934. For his campaign, he released the utopian novel titled *I, Governor of California, and How I Ended Poverty: A True Story of the Future.* Horrified at a Socialist-leaning candidate, the Republicans launched a vitriolic counter-campaign, including faked news footage of crazed bums flocking to California to "launch the Sinclair revolution." Republican incumbent Frank Merriam defeated Sinclair.

Earl Warren, Future Chief Justice of the U.S. Supreme Court

In 1946, Earl Warren had the unusual honor of not only winning the nomination for governor from his own party, the Republicans, but from the Democrats and Progressives as well. As a result, he was the only governor in California's history to run for re-election unopposed. Warren's huge popularity in office gained him an unprecedented third term in 1950. President Dwight Eisenhower appointed Warren chief justice of the U.S. Supreme Court in 1952. Warren's judgments are credited with helping move civil rights forward in the decades that followed.

Ronald Reagan

Ronald Reagan defeated incumbent Edmund G. "Pat" Brown for the California governorship in 1966. In the wake of the Watts Riots in L.A., in which 34 people died and hundreds of millions of dollars of property was destroyed, Reagan's campaign promise to restore order appealed to many California voters.

Glide Memorial Church and the Reverend Cecil Williams

San Francisco's Glide Memorial Church is famous for its rocking, jazz-filled services and for its outspoken minister of more than 30 years, the Reverend Cecil Williams. When Williams came to the church in 1963, he started by removing the cross from the sanctuary, insisting that people celebrate life instead. "We must all be the cross," he said. He welcomed marginalized groups—hippies, gays, drug addicts and the poor—into the church.

Angela Davis

A lecturer in philosophy at UC Berkeley in the 1960s, Angela Davis was fired in 1970 for her Communist Party affiliation. While working to improve conditions for prison inmates, Davis was charged by the FBI for allegedly conspiring to murder a prison guard. Although she was acquitted, then-Governor Ronald Reagan barred her from teaching at a state university. When the ban was eventually lifted, Davis was hired to lecture at San Francisco State and wrote numerous books. In 1980 and 1984, she was the vice-presidential candidate for the American Communist Party.

DID YOU KNOW?

Born in the Central Valley town of Oakdale, Dr. March Fong Eu was the first woman to serve (1974 to 1994) as California Secretary of State and the first Asian American in any constitutional office in the state.

Kook or Visionary?

San Francisco–born Edmund G. "Jerry" Brown Jr., was voted into California's governorship in 1974 at the age of 34. Brown refused many of the trappings of his office, preferring a modest apartment to the posh Governor's Mansion and turning down chauffeured limousines in favor of a Plymouth Satellite from the state vehicle pool. Brown was re-elected in 1978. After some failed attempts to win national political office, he served as mayor of Oakland from 1998 to 2006 and then won the state's attorney general position.

DID YOU  KNOW?

California's Executive Mansion was sold during Jerry Brown's governorship and is now a state park. Built in Sacramento in 1877, the mansion housed a series of 13 governors until 1967. Ronald Reagan was the last governor to live in the house. The sumptuous abode has 14-foot ceilings in its more than 30 rooms, all decked out with chandeliers, French mirrors and fireplaces made of Italian marble.

Harvey Milk

In 1977, San Franciscans elected Harvey Milk to their city Board of Supervisors. Milk was the first openly gay person to hold public office in the state. Among other acts, Milk arranged baseball games between members of the gay community and members of the famously homophobic San Francisco police force to ease tensions between the two groups and help end police harassment of gays. Tragically, former city supervisor Dan White shot Milk to death in November 1978.

DID YOU KNOW?

Senator Barbara Boxer's daughter was married (for six years) to Hillary Rodham Clinton's brother. Does that make them senators-in-law?

Mr. Speaker

Willie Brown was the first African-American speaker of the California State Assembly, serving from 1980 to 1995, becoming the state's longest-serving speaker. He later served as mayor of San Francisco from 1996 to 2004.

Democratic Women at the Helm

At a national level, California is currently run by female Democrats.

☛ U.S. Senator Dianne Feinstein, who was previously San Francisco's first (and only) female mayor, has held office since 1992.

☛ Barbara Boxer started her political career in Marin County and served 10 years as a U.S. Rep. before being elected to the Senate in 1993.

Speaker Pelosi: A Lot of Firsts

Nancy Pelosi, U.S. Rep. from San Francisco's 8th District, became the first woman Speaker of the U.S. House of Representatives in 2007. This position puts her second only to Vice-President Dick Cheney in the presidential line of succession. Pelosi is also the first Italian American—and the first Californian—to hold that office.

UNDERGROUND MOVEMENTS

Chinese Exclusion

By 1852, an estimated 25,000 Chinese people had come to California, either as gold miners or laborers on the transcontinental railroad. During an economic downturn in the 1870s, anti-Chinese rhetoric grew among white working men who blamed the Chinese for their unemployment.

An 1877 meeting of the Workingmen's Party in San Francisco turned violent when rowdies stirred up antagonism against the Chinese. The ensuing riot wrecked Chinese laundries. The police tried to stop the rioters, as did a citizens group called the "Committee of Safety," but rioting continued for three nights, leaving many laundries destroyed, buildings of the Pacific Mail Steamship Company (that transported Chinese immigrants) burned and several people dead.

The Wobblies

The Industrial Workers of the World (IWW), nicknamed the "Wobblies," organized California workers on farms and in factories, starting in 1905. IWW clashes with police led to the Wheatland riot in 1913, in which several people were killed. The National Guard ran the IWW out of the Sacramento Valley. The 1919 Criminal Syndicalism Law made the Wobblies and other unions illegal for a time.

San Francisco General Strike

Discontented workers formed a vigorous labor movement in the 1930s. Andrew Furuseth and Harry Bridges headed up the International Longshoremen's Association on the San Francisco waterfront. It was the San Francisco longshoremen who led the great strike of 1934 that halted work for 90 days on docks from San Diego to Seattle, Washington.

The State of Jefferson

The idea of separating northern from southern California has been bandied about since the state's inception. One of the quirkier instances occurred in 1941, when a group from four northern counties leafleted motorists with plans to become the separate state of Jefferson. The flyer handed out near Yreka, the proposed state capital, read: "Patriotic Jeffersonians intend to secede each Thursday until further notice."

Farm Workers Unite

Central Valley residents Delores Huerta and Cesar Chavez co-organized the United Farm Workers (UFW)—the first successful farm workers' union in U.S. history.

Black Panthers

The Oakland-born Black Panthers organization was a source of pride for many African Americans in the 1960s, with 2000 members in a number of cities. Inspired by Malcolm X, co-founders Huey P. Newton and Bobby Seale urged black Americans to arm themselves in self-defense against police brutality and other injustices. The Panthers' militarism, however, alienated many moderate blacks and whites.

Free Speech

When the UC Berkeley administration decided in 1964 to for-bid political advocacy on campus, a coalition of 18 organizations calling themselves the Free Speech Movement protested. The broad coalition included not just the Independent Socialist Club but also the University Young Republicans.

Anti-Vietnam War Protests

On April 15, 1967, 100,000 people marched to Golden Gate Park to protest the Vietnam War. That year, folksinger Joan Baez hit international news when she was arrested for sitting-in at an East Bay military induction center, and thousands in Oakland poured into the streets and clashed with police during the largest anti-Vietnam War protest to date.

Un-Thanksgiving

On November 20, 1969, approximately 90 Native Americans, most of them college students, occupied Alcatraz Island in the San Francisco Bay for 19 months, claiming it (or reclaiming it) as Native American land. The occupation helped empower the newly formed American Indian Movement (AIM) across the country.

Gay Rights

The rather stuffy-sounding Council on Religion and the Homosexual (CRH), a group of liberal ministers who felt that gay individuals should have equal rights, organized a gay-oriented New Year's Eve Ball in 1965. At the time, police harassment of the gay community was a major issue. True to form, San Francisco Police showed up at the 1965 ball and arrested several of the ministers. The arrests led to public outcry and served as a watershed in gay rights.

PHOTOGRAPHERS, PAINTERS AND SCULPTORS

The Society of Six

"The Society of Six," a group of Northern California landscape painters—Louis Bassi Siegriest, Maurice George Logan, William Henry Clapp, August Francois Gay, Selden Conner Gile and Bernard James von Eichman—worked together from 1917 to 1928 in Oakland, revolutionizing *plein air* painting.

For the Love of Yosemite

Born and raised in San Francisco, Ansel Adams (1902–84) fell in love with Yosemite when his parents took him there on a family vacation in 1916 at the age of 14 and gave him a Kodak Box Brownie camera. Adams' subsequent career helped define American photography with his striking black-and-white images of the natural world.

DID YOU KNOW?

Fresno-born painter Maynard Dixon, famed for his depiction of the U.S. West, was married for 15 years to Dorothea Lange, noted documentary photographer.

Documenting People's Lives

Dorothea Lange (1895–1965) started as a commercial photographer in 1920s San Francisco. In 1935, she launched the work for which she is best remembered, documenting the lives of the destitute farmers who came westward in the wake of the Dust Bowl. Her photographs helped motivate the government to provide assistance for the disadvantaged. Today the largest collection of Lange's photographs is at the Oakland Museum.

DID YOU  KNOW?

Northern California's Pomo tribe, residing in the Russian River basin, were masters of basketry. Made in a great variety of shapes and decorated in intricate geometric patterns, their baskets were often bright with feathers and beads.

Rivera Murals

In 1931, renowned Mexican muralist Diego Rivera visited the Bay Area with his wife, painter Frida Kahlo. That year, he completed two commissions, *Allegory of California* in the San Francisco Stock Exchange Building and *The Making of a Fresco, Showing the Building of a City* at the California School of Fine Arts (now San Francisco Art Institute). In 1940, Rivera painted *Pan American Unity* at San Francisco City College.

DID YOU  KNOW?

California's most prominent sculptor, Douglas Tilden (1860–1935), lost his hearing during a bout of scarlet fever at age four. His sculptures stand at the Champs Elysees in Paris and throughout his native San Francisco.

Charged Topics

Sculptor George Segal (1924–2000) was not averse to controversy. His *The Holocaust, 1984* in San Francisco's Lincoln Park depicts human bodies stretched and piled on the ground beside a section of barbed-wire. His 1994 piece *Gay Liberation* in Palo Alto portrays two same-sex couples.

Coit Tower Uproar

In 1934, the opening of San Francisco's Coit Memorial Tower on the crest of Telegraph Hill became the scene of picketing, censorship and furor. The tower had been chosen as the site for murals depicting the "American scene in all its aspects."

A preview of the new murals, however, revealed that the painters had added a copy of Karl Marx's *Das Kapital*, the Communist Party publication *New Masses* and a hammer-and-sickle emblem. The San Francisco Parks Commission closed the tower. The public picketed, and police put up a police line. The Art Commission voted to remove the more flagrant Communist icons, and, in October 1934, the tower opened without further incident.

DID YOU KNOW?

The Cantor Art Center at Stanford University has the largest collection of bronze sculptures by Rodin anywhere outside of Paris. The collection includes a model of *The Thinker* and *The Gates of Hell*.

The Birth Project

Artist Judy Chicago, known for the multimedia *Dinner Party* that highlighted important women throughout history, chose the small town of Benicia, just north of Berkeley, as headquarters for *The Birth Project*, which used the traditionally female media of fabric and needlework to depict beautiful and sometimes shocking images of women giving birth.

MUSIC

San Francisco's "First Concert"

The first concert in Northern California took place at San Francisco's Old Police Court on June 22, 1849.

A Symphony Rises from the Ashes

The Great Earthquake of 1906 stalled plans for a symphony in San Francisco. Five years later, the city's civic-minded citizens finally succeeded in launching the San Francisco Symphony, which played its first concert in December 1911.

Nashville West

When the Dust Bowl of the 1930s chased thousands from southern states out to California, the "Okies"—the name is a short form of Oklahoma—brought their culture with them and started up dancehalls and honky-tonks. Bakersfield came to be known as

"Nashville West" for launching the careers of such country music stars as Buck Owens, Glen Campbell and Merle Haggard.

Northern California's Rock Scene

Rock 'n' roll culture exploded in the Bay Area in the mid-1960s.

☛ A new Bay Area band, Jefferson Airplane (formerly The Great Society and later, Jefferson Starship), performed at San Francisco's first folk nightclub, The Matrix, in 1965.

☛ Pandemonium broke out and fans rushed the stage when the Beatles played at the Cow Palace in Daly City in 1965.

☛ A group called The Warlocks decided to change their name in 1965 and played for the first time as The Grateful Dead at San Francisco's Fillmore West.

☛ A gutsy little singer joined the band Big Brother and The Holding Company in concert for the first time on June 10, 1966 at the Avalon Ballroom. The audience loved Janis Joplin.

☛ Creedence Clearwater Revival, at first called The Blue Velvets and later The Golliwogs, got its start in El Cerrito in 1958 as the "house" rock band for Portola Jr. High. In 1969, their song "Proud Mary" became a monster hit.

☛ A chance 1966 meeting in San Francisco between Carlos Santana and keyboardist Gregg Rolie spawned the band Santana.

☛ The first, last and only Monterey International Pop Festival in June 1967 has become legend for its gut-wrenching, blazing (literally) performances, including that of Jefferson Airplane, Otis Redding, The Who, Janis Joplin and Jimi Hendrix.

 CLASSIC CALIFORNIA

The last public appearance of The Beatles together was in San Francisco's Candlestick Park on August 29, 1966.

Violin With a History

The concert master of the San Francisco Symphony plays the "David Guarnerius del Gesu" violin, which virtuoso Jascha Heifetz played in nearly every performance and recording of his career.

A Warning

Famous folk songwriter Woody Guthrie, of "This Land Is Your Land" fame, was born in Oklahoma. Like other Okies, he traveled to California in 1937, hoping for a brighter future. Guthrie's lyrics in the song "Do Re Mi" warned of the hardships ahead for poor immigrants:

California is a garden of Eden,
A paradise to live in or see
But believe it or not, you won't find it so hot
If you ain't got the do re mi.

1960s Folk Music

In the 1960s, Northern California residents such as Joan Baez, Malvina Reynolds, Richard Fariña and Baez's little sis Mimi Fariña gave new life to traditional folk music.

Creedence Who?

Not many people know that Creedence Clearwater Revival headlined at the famous Woodstock concert partly because the group played after The Grateful Dead, which put them on stage at three o'clock in the morning. Even the owls were asleep by then. What's more, the band members nixed themselves from the film because they didn't like their performance (at 3:00 AM, who could blame them?), and a dispute over rights kept their songs off the film soundtrack as well.

DID YOU  **KNOW?**

Creedence Clearwater Revival reportedly cobbled their band name together—after they wisely deep-sixed the name The Golliwogs—from a friend's weird name (Credence Nuball), a beer commercial (Clearwater) and the desire for long-sought-after fame (Revival).

ARCHITECTURE

Picturesque to the Nth Degree

In 1885, William Carson, lumber magnate of Eureka, hired San Francisco architects Samuel and Joseph Newson to design a mansion in the Picturesque style. The home took more than 100 laborers over two years to complete. In addition to using the local redwood, Carson imported 97,000 board feet of white mahogany from Central America and wood from Mexico, India and the Philippines. Today, the William Carson House stands on Eureka's M Street.

Palace of Fine Arts

When San Francisco hosted the World's Fair in 1915, architects designed more than 100 temporary buildings that were not meant to last. The city did opt to build one structure intended to endure: the Palace of Fine Arts, designed by noted architect and UC Berkeley professor Bernard R. Maybeck. The stately Mediterranean-style building now houses the Exploratorium Museum.

The World's Fair of 1915

The Panama Pacific International Exposition—or World's Fair—in San Francisco in 1915 changed forever the art world's impression of California artists. Architects designed a series of buildings for the Fair, and artists created 1500 sculptures and murals. One critic commented, "…the future of art belongs to the West."

Part of the Fair was the Tower of Jewels, a 43-story showpiece covered with 100,000 colored-glass shards that flashed as the breeze moved through.

Yabba Dabba Doo

The so-called "Flintstones' House" sits along Highway 280 in Hillsborough. Also called the "mushroom house" or the "dome house," the bulbous white residence was designed in 1976 by architect William Nicholson and built of concrete sprayed over giant aeronautical balloons. Neighbors were so horrified at how the structure looked that they founded an architectural review board to prevent any more such oddities from being built.

Julia Morgan

Architect Julia Morgan (1872–1957) is probably most famous for designing the Hearst Castle at San Simeon and the Berkeley City Club. After growing up in Oakland, Morgan received her BS in civil engineering from UC Berkeley before traveling overseas to study at Paris' famed École de Beaux-Arts as the school's first female student. She returned to Oakland and, when the Great Earthquake struck, helped to reconstruct the area's buildings, including repairing the Fairmont Hotel.

Employees who work in the Transamerica Pyramid in San Francisco call it the "Zippy the Pinhead Building" because the comic strip character was reputed to live in a room at the top.

Frank Lloyd Wright

Architect Frank Lloyd Wright (1867–1959) worked his magic throughout Northern California with 13 buildings completed, the most famous of which is the Marin County Civic Center, just north of San Rafael, with its long low lines, pastel palette and domed blue roofs. Wright also created Stanford University's hexagonal Hanna House and the Pilgrim Congregational Church in Redding. He designed the 1950 Robert Berger House in San Anselmo, which comes complete with a Wright-designed one-of-a-kind doghouse.

In the pre-1937 heyday of the Hearst family estate, the Hearst Castle had its own private zoo, housing, among other exotic animals, camels, kangaroos and grizzly bears.

LITERATURE

Famous for Frogs

One of America's literary treasures, Mark Twain set his famous 1867 short story "The Celebrated Jumping Frog of Calaveras County" in northern California. The real Calaveras County holds an annual Jumping Frog Jubilee. In 2002, the contest had more than 2000 competitors, with the current record held by Rosie the Ribeter, who sprang 21 feet and 5 inches.

DID YOU KNOW?

Ina Coolbrith was California's first poet laureate in 1915. Coolbrith, a San Francisco resident since 1862, was friends with fellow writers Mark Twain and Bret Harte, and, as librarian of the Oakland Free Library, mentored a young, impoverished waif named Jack London.

Our Favorite Dropout

One young man from a working family in Salinas attended Stanford University in 1919. He barely got by with a C in freshman English and dropped out two years later. The same fellow tried again in 1923, with journalism, only to drop out again. In 1962, the Nobel Committee saw fit to award this loser the Nobel Prize in Literature. I guess John Steinbeck did okay when he wrote *Grapes of Wrath*, which won the 1940 Pulitzer Prize, *East of Eden* and *Of Mice and Men*.

Those Merry Pranksters

The Beatniks, or "Beats," made a significant mark on 1950s and '60s Northern California. It was while a student at Stanford University that Ken Kesey volunteered for psychology department experiments involving psilocybin, mescaline and LSD. (Ah, those were the days!) One of Kesey's hallucinations inspired him to write his fiction masterpiece *One Flew Over the Cuckoo's Nest*. Funds from *Cuckoo's Nest* bought the now-famous psychedelic school bus that carried the "Merry Pranksters" (Jack Kerouac and company) from San Francisco to New York for the World's Fair. Kesey's LSD experience also led him to host wild parties, which were called "Acid Tests."

Lawrence Ferlinghetti founded City Lights Bookstore in San Francisco as the first all-paperbound bookshop in the nation.

Cleaver on Ice

Eldridge Cleaver spent most of his young life in jail. He used his time under lock and key to educate himself, and eventually he put together a collection of essays that made a lasting mark on history. Cleaver's 1968 book *Soul on Ice* became a classic for its portrayal of the alienation African Americans felt in the U.S.

Milosz

The Lithuanian-born Czeslaw Milosz spent the last 40 years of his life in Berkeley as a professor of Slavic languages and literature at the University of California. The celebrated poet was awarded the Nobel Prize in Literature in 1980.

The Color Purple

Alice Walker, the eighth child of Georgia sharecroppers, was awarded the Pulitzer Prize in 1983 for her novel *The Color Purple*. The book was made into a Steven Spielberg film that starred (among others) Oprah Winfrey. Nowadays, Walker lives in a remote valley inland of Mendocino.

Amy Tan

Born in Oakland in 1952, Amy Tan grew up the child of Chinese immigrant parents. Her 1989 novel *The Joy Luck Club*, which reflected this experience, became a surprise bestseller, spending more than 40 weeks on the *New York Times* bestseller list.

Zen Beat Naturalist Poet

Born in San Francisco in 1930, Gary Snyder worked as a logger and seaman on a Pacific tanker. He studied Oriental languages at UC Berkeley in the 1950s, hung with fellow Beats Ginsberg and Kerouac and studied Buddhism in Japan. His collection of poetry *Turtle Island* won the 1975 Pulitzer Prize. These days Snyder teaches poetry and "wilderness thought" at UC Davis and lives in Grass Valley.

California's First Book

Augustin V. Zamorano published the state's first book in 1834. In 1849, Washington Bartlett, who later served as San Francisco's mayor and the state's governor, published the state's first book printed in English.

Those Lazy Locals

Richard Henry Dana, who wrote the classic novel *Two Years Before the Mast*, shipped aboard the *Pilgrim* in 1835 for 18 months along the California coast. A New Englander, Dana thought the local population lazy. "In the hands of an enterprising people," he commented in his journals, "what a country this might be!"

The Ferlinghetti Trial

Lawrence Ferlinghetti, Beat poet and founder of City Lights Bookstore in San Francisco, was arrested on obscenity charges when he published Allen Ginsberg's 1956 poem *Howl*. His trial and eventual acquittal brought national attention to censorship issues and to what was later termed the San Francisco literary renaissance.

Fishing At Home

Jack London, well known for his *Call of the Wild* and other novels, planned to have his dream house built near Glen Ellen in 1911. The four-story, $80,000 structure featured, among other luxuries, a pool stocked with bass.

Sisyphus West

For five years, poet Robinson Jeffers rolled boulders up by hand from the beach below his house in Carmel to build the 40-foot-tall "Hawk Tower." Of the tower, Jeffers observed, "I hung stone in the sky."

Joan Didion

From Sacramento came one of the nation's most astute observers of modern politics and culture. Joan Didion, born in 1934, took her BA from UC Berkeley. Some of her more famous works include two collections of essays, *Slouching Toward Bethlehem* (1968) and *The White Album* (1979). Her 2005 memoir *A Year of Magical Thinking* won the National Book Award.

More on Eldridge Cleaver

Upon his release from prison, Cleaver spent some time working with the Black Panthers in Oakland. These days, reports are that Mr. Cleaver has become a born-again Christian and a card-carrying Republican. It's a long and winding road, indeed.

Rancher Nurses

The Scottish novelist and poet Robert Louis Stevenson was nursed back to health by a group of ranchers in Monterey. The writer's delicate health had been battered by an overland voyage from New York to California as he made his way to see his future wife, Fanny Vandegrift Osbourne, in San Francisco. When he recovered, Stevenson and Osbourne wed and honeymooned in the Napa area.

Obscene or Literary?

The troubled and troubling, if quintessentially American, works of author Henry Miller include *Tropic of Cancer* and *Tropic of Capricorn*. The U.S. publication of *Tropic of Cancer* in 1961 led to obscenity charges that made their way to the Supreme Court. After traveling and befriending many notable literary figures (including a famous love affair with Anaïs Nin), Miller settled in Big Sur in 1944. Here he lived almost 20 years and wrote many works, including *Big Sur and the Oranges of Hieronymus Bosch*.

A Modern Immigrant's Tales

Maxine Hong Kingston grew up in Stockton, but her first language was one that many Californians have probably never even heard of. Say Yup is a dialect of Cantonese. Kingston's parents had immigrated to America from China before her birth. The girl who grew up with a love of language and storytelling went on to win the National Book Critics Award for Nonfiction not once but twice, for *The Woman Warrior* in 1976 and *China Men* in 1980. Her 1988 novel *Tripmaster Monkey: His Fake Book* is set in San Francisco in the 1960s. While her books stand alone as literature, Kingston's work also teaches others about the experience of Chinese immigrants in the U.S.

MEDIA AND ENTERTAINMENT

Bilingual Newspaper

California's first recorded bilingual newspaper started publication in 1846. The weekly *Monterey Californian* was put out half in Spanish, half in English by Commodore Stockton.

State's First Daily Newspaper

California's first daily, the *Alta California*, started publication in January 1849. *Alta*, meaning upper, distinguishes the state from "lower," or *Baja*, California, which remained part of Mexico after the Mexican-American War.

It Wasn't the Chronicle

In January 1847, San Francisco's first newspaper, the *California Star*, was published.

Gold Fever

On May 29, 1848, the *Californian* newspaper lamented, "The whole country from San Francisco to Los Angeles, and from the sea shore to the base of the Sierra Nevadas, resounds with the sordid cry of 'gold, GOLD, GOLD!' while the field is left half-planted, the house half built, and everything neglected but the manufacture of shovels and pickaxes." Just two weeks later, however, on June 14, the paper had to cease publication because its staff had left for the gold fields.

Sacramento's First Paper

The *Placer Times*, Sacramento's first newspaper, started rolling off the press at Sutter's Fort on April 28, 1849.

Life of Leisure

The first issue of *Sunset* magazine was put out in 1898 by the Southern Pacific Company's Passenger Department to promote "settlement, travel and investment" in the states the railroad rolled through.

Counterculture

The counterculture *Berkeley Barb* started in 1965 on the UC Berkeley campus, as a chronicle of the civil rights and anti-war movements. Distributed on street corners by flower children, the *Barb* folded in 1970. The *Guardian*, which debuted in 1966, has survived and continues in print today.

A Short-lived Debut

California's first theater, the Eagle Theatre, opened on Front
Street in Sacramento on October 18, 1849. Alas, the Great
Flood of 1850 washed it away just four months later.

Dangerous Mimes

In 1965, San Francisco's Parks Commission denied the San
Francisco Mime Troupe a permit to perform in Lafayette Park,
dubbing its material "not fit for consumption." The troupe performed anyway, and police tossed the group's leader, R.G. Davis,
in jail. (He was later released.) The Mime Troupe (sans Davis)
went on to win two *Village Voice* Obie Awards and become the
subject of the 1985 documentary *Troupers*. In 1987, the group
received a Tony Award for outstanding regional theater.

Buried Child

Sam Shepard's 1979 play *Buried Child* propelled its author into
national prominence, winning him a Pulitzer Prize, and was the
first play to be thus honored that had not yet opened on Broadway.
Shepard premiered the show at the Magic Theater in San
Francisco's Fort Mason during his five years as playwright-in-
residence there.

Ancient Theater in a Logging Town

The tiny logging town of Blue Lake, tucked away in the far
Northern California hills, is home to an unlikely resident—the
Dell'Arte International School of Physical Theatre. Started in 1974,
the school is now an internationally renowned training program
for physical theater and is arguably the best in the country.

Marin County Film Empire

In 1973, a guy named George Lucas set up shop in Marin
County and made a movie for $750,000 (chicken scratch in the
film world) in spite of nay-saying film execs. The film, *American
Graffiti,* took in $100 million worldwide, received five Academy
Award nominations and launched the careers of Richard
Dreyfuss, Suzanne Somers, Ron Howard and Harrison Ford.

Lucas went on to produce the *Star Wars* and *Lord of the Rings* films.
The first *Star Wars* film, released in 1977, is the largest grossing
film ever and won eight Academy Awards. These days Lucas
maintains the somewhat-secret Skywalker Ranch near Nicasio and
Lucasfilm's digital arts center in San Francisco's Presidio.

Skywalker Ranch

Filmmaker George
Lucas has estab-
lished a "secret"
estate for himself
and his crew—no
one else allowed—
in Marin County's
rolling rural hills
somewhere near
Nicasio (it's said).
Ninety-eight per-
cent of the ranch is
dedicated to the
Marin Agricultural
Land Trust, to
prove what a nice

guy Mr. Lucas is, I guess. Which he does seem to be, at least in
that department. The *Wall Street Journal* estimates the spread
cost Lucas about $100 million, which, if you think about it, is
a heck of a lot of Wookie action figures.

Whenever there's a secret, stories grow up around it. One story about Skywalker Ranch is that when Lucasfilm lost their court battle to have the Reagan government stop calling its strategic defense initiative "Star Wars," the president requested a tour of Lucas' ranch. No hard feelings, right? Wrong! Permission denied. The force, in that case, was decidedly against Bonzo's old buddy.

Movie Locations

Northern California offers many sought-after locations for filming. These movies were filmed there:

The Birds: Alfred Hitchcock filmed this 1963 classic largely in the little coastal town of Bodega.

Vertigo: Hitchcock set this dizzying 1958 film in the steep streets of San Francisco. In one scene, detective Scottie Ferguson (James Stewart) tracks Madeleine Elster (Kim Novak) into the Mission Delores cemetery where she places flowers on a grave.

The Love Bug: Filmed in 1968, brave little Herbie the VW Bug makes his way down the zigzags of San Francisco's Lombard Street.

American Graffiti: George Lucas' 1973 breakout film was inspired by the director's teenage years spent cruising Highway 99 out of Modesto. The towns where the film was made, San Rafael and Petaluma, however, had better-preserved cruising strips. The high school in the film is Tamalpais High in Mill Valley.

Rebel Without a Cause: The young star of this 1955 film was on his way to an auto race in Salinas when he got into a fatal highway accident. James Dean's famous death took place in Cholame, a town inland of San Luis Obispo, on September 30, 1955.

Star Trek IV: The Voyage Home: Captain Kirk and his crew "return" to the distant past (a.k.a. 1986) to save the humpback whales. Spock hangs out in the Bay Area streets in his bathrobe wearing a headband and no one bats an eye.

Movies With the Golden Gate Bridge

The Golden Gate Bridge crops up in films throughout history. Here are some examples:

It Came From Beneath the Sea (1955): A giant octopus wreaks all kinds of havoc.

A View to a Kill (1985): James Bond clambers about in an unsafe way on the bridge as he tries to stop the evil guy who wants to destroy Silicon Valley. (Did Bond have stock in Apple or what?)

Star Trek VI: The Undiscovered Country (1991): Kirk, Spock and friends defend a peace treaty from their Star Fleet Academy at the Golden Gate Bridge.

Interview with a Vampire (1994): Tom Cruise and Brad Pitt bare their fangs as they cruise (pun intended) across the famous bridge.

INVENTIONS, DISCOVERIES AND BREAKTHROUGHS

First In Flight?

While most people consider the Wright brothers to be the first in flight, one Grass Valley resident begged to differ. Lyman Gilmore got airborne in 1891. That was in an 18-foot glider pulled by a horse that (understandably) got spooked by the contraption. Gilmore decided he could do better. He built a 32-foot, steam-powered plane he claimed he flew in May 1902. Although that was a year before the Wright brothers' famed ascent, there were few witnesses to confirm Gilmore's feat.

First on a Snowplow

But, wait! There's more. Gilmore lived a quirky life, full of (mostly mis-) adventures. In addition to an airplane, he invented an early version of the rotary snowplow, designed to get snow off the railroad tracks. The railroads were interested and offered Gilmore $10,000 for his invention. When he held out for

$20,000, however, the railroads came up with their own version of the machine, and Gilmore ended up with nothing. Poor sod!

Liar, Liar!

You've probably always wondered who invented the "cardio-pneumo-psychogram." Well, it was John Larson, a medical student who sidelined as an employee of the Berkeley police in the 1920s. The tongue-twisting moniker was his own name for the device; others call it a "polygraph" or, even more commonly, a lie detector. Other lie detectors had been invented as early as 1902, but Larson is credited with creating the modern version used in forensic science. Larson's device measures respiratory rates, blood pressure and pulse and records them on a drum of paper. The question is, how does a medical student have time to work for the police department?

First in the Jacuzzi

Born on a farm in Italy in 1903, Candido Jacuzzi probably never thought, "I'll bet I'm going to invent a device that will be used in hot tubs across California." Jacuzzi immigrated to the U.S. in 1920 and settled in Berkeley. It was the pain caused by his child's arthritis that inspired the father in 1949 to design a submersible pump that created a soothing whirlpool in the bathtub. He patented his creation, and the family business began to manufacture the J-300 hydrotherapy pump and sell it to hospitals and schools.

According to the current Jacuzzi website, Candido and his seven brothers also invented the first enclosed-cabin monoplane, which was used to deliver U.S. mail and transport passengers from San Francisco to the newly created Yosemite National Park.

Square Tomatoes

First, we need to note (duly) that the famed "square tomatoes" are not really square. Sorry. Even so, you may curse their founder, since they are tough little numbers. Gordie "Jack"

Hanna (1938–67), a researcher at UC Davis, set out in the 1950s to solve the dilemma of commercial farms that wanted to harvest tomatoes with a newly invented (and oh-so-spiffy) mechanical harvester. Trouble was that the harvester mashed the tender tomatoes to a pulp. Hanna's goal was to develop a breed of tomatoes sturdy enough to withstand the punishment the harvester delivered. For his research, or so the story goes, he stood in the tomato field and threw random tomatoes onto the nearby road. Those that didn't smoosh, he kept. Thanks to Hanna, today's tomatoes are harvested in one piece by machines just as he hoped, and they are tough as shoe leather.

Mail Service

While tens of thousands of Americans flooded into California after the discovery of gold in 1848, the infrastructure lagged a bit. Pony Express mail service began in 1860, but it was a rough trip from the East Coast in those days and the service was minimal.

Dot Dot Dash

Telegraph "instant" communication between California and the rest of the country started when the wires were set in 1861.

"Wireless" in the Old Sense

The first time "wireless"—we're talking radio here, not Internet—was used on the west coast of the U.S. was in August 1899, when the troopship *Sherman* came in towards the San Francisco Bay.

Cable Cars

Anyone who has been to San Francisco has experienced the city's precipitous streets. It hurts just to walk up some of them. Imagine, then, trying to haul a wagon of goods up one of those streets on a rainy day. In the 1860s, Andrew Smith Hallidie watched a horse struggle to pull a horsecar up the wet cobblestones of Jackson Street. As Hallidie watched, the car driver whipped the horses mercilessly until they slipped and were dragged to their deaths down the hill.

Hallidie was moved by the incident to design what became the city's cable cars. Hallidie used a "wire rope" his father had patented in Great Britain (the inventor bug ran in the family) to come up with a way to pull train-like cars up the steep grades. The cable was centrally powered by a steam engine. Hallidie tested the first cable car at 4:00 AM on August 2, 1873, on Clay Street. The "Clay Street Hill Railroad" started service the next month and was a huge success.

Shake, Rattle and Roll

I guess necessity really is the mother of invention. It certainly follows, then, that the tool for measuring the magnitude of an earthquake originated in California. This one came from Southern California but, since earthquakes are one thing that unites both regions (so to speak), it seems right to mention them here.

Charles F. Richter developed the Richter magnitude scale in 1935 while at the California Institute of Technology in Pasadena. The scale, for you math nerds, is based on a logarithm. What this means is that each whole number increase—from 5.0 to 6.0, for example—indicates a tenfold increase in size. So while 5.0 feels like your washer has gone into the spin cycle; 6.0 will rattle the dentures right out of your mouth. Something like that.

DID YOU KNOW?

The U.S. Navy has never been known for its aesthetic sense. If it had had its way, the Golden Gate Bridge would be painted an oh-so-attractive black with yellow stripes. That would, they argue, offer greater visibility to passing ships.

A Tunnel for Toads

The town that brought you square tomatoes has also innovated in the unlikely area of toad assistance. In 1995, the city of Davis spent $14,000 to construct a tunnel to help toads, hopping across a stretch of Interstate 80, get safely to the other side. (Hold all the chicken jokes, please.) The tunnel is 21 inches wide and 18 inches tall. Like all innovations, this one required some refinement. The toads refused to use the new-fangled tunnel until lights were installed. Then there was one more glitch: local toad-eating birds caught on to the steady supply of toad snacks emerging from the tunnel's exit. Perhaps to give the toads a way to dodge the birds (it's not really clear), a local postmaster constructed a miniature village at the tunnel's mouth complete with—of course—a post office.

Bridging the Bay

When the San Francisco-Oakland Bay Bridge was built in 1936, it was the world's longest steel bridge. The bridge's opening festivities included the release of 1500 pigeons (I hope hats were recommended) and a skywriter etching "The bridge is open" overhead.

The Golden Gate

Construction began in 1933 on what is today one of Northern California's iconic structures—the Golden Gate Bridge. With a central span 4200 feet long and the tallest towers (746 feet high) in the world at that time, the Golden Gate bore the title of longest suspension bridge in the world for 27 years. In 1964, the Verrazano Narrows Bridge in New York exceeded the span by 60 feet and walked away with the prize, which has since passed to other contenders.

Lives Lost

Eleven workers lost their lives while building the Golden Gate Bridge. After the first death, a safety net was suspended under the floor of the bridge from one end to the other. No more builders died from falling, except for the time that 10 fatalities happened all at once when a section of scaffold carrying 12 men fell through the safety net. Amazingly, two of them survived the fall.

DID YOU KNOW?

How many vehicles have gone across the Golden Gate Bridge? As of June 2005, that would be 1,779,032,891 since the bridge opened in 1937.

The Halfway-to-Hell Club

Tough conditions bring out dark humor. Workers building the Golden Gate Bridge dealt with strong winds, precarious perches and the sight of the roiling water below them in the San Francisco Bay. In fact, the bridge's engineer, Joseph Straus, later described the conditions in this way, "I know of no place on the globe which has more violent conditions of water and weather than the Golden Gate." So it was in this setting that, during construction, 19 men slipped from the bridge but—instead of falling to their deaths in the waters below, as 11 others did—were rescued by the safety net. These fellows became known as the "Halfway-to-Hell Club."

DID YOU  KNOW?

The cultural icon and multimillion-dollar endeavor of eBay was originally founded to trade Pez dispensers. You know, those little plastic candy holders with the various cute heads on them.

High Tech from a Small Town

A prominent filmmaking technology company got its start in the to-all-appearances-decidedly-low-tech Grass Valley in 1958. The aptly titled Grass Valley Group designs and manufactures digital cinema products with names such as the "MPEG-2 Toolkit" that are way too complicated for the average person to understand. Such equipment has proved crucial, however, for major Hollywood films such as the Star Wars prequel *The Phantom Menace* (1999).

Mousing Around

While working in his lab at Stanford, Douglas Engelbart created the first computer mouse. He received a patent in 1970 for the gadget, which he described as an "X-Y position indicator for a display system." The first prototype was a wooden shell with two metal wheels. Engelbart called his invention a mouse (before anyone else could) "because the tail came out the end." Okay. He hadn't exactly set out to design a mouse. Engelbart was bent on creating a hypermedia groupware system called NLS (for oNLine System). Don't ask me what that is. Never mind. The guy was brilliant. With his help, we all surf the Web a little more easily. He holds 45 other patents as well. In 1995, *Byte* magazine named Engelbart as one of the 20 people who have had the greatest impact on personal computing.

DID YOU  KNOW?

If we were to build the Golden Gate Bridge today. it would cost an estimated $1.2 billion.

Is It Still Foggy Out?

Observations of San Francisco's weather (foggy) began in 1849, when nautical-instrument-maker Thomas Tennent set up a rain gauge on the northeast corner of Union and (what is now) Grant Streets. He kept daily track of rainfall, along with data on the sunrise, sunset, tides and earthquakes for 22 years. Although he sounds like an obsessive oddball (I bet he drove his wife crazy), Tennent rose to prominence in the city, serving three terms on the Board of Supervisors and designing the house-numbering system that remains in use today for much of the city.

San Francisco's First Fire Engine

The "Martin Van Buren" engine arrived on December 9, 1849 from the East Coast. The engine was named after the president because it had supposedly been used to water the lawn at his New York estate. In fact, the truck had not been intended for use on fires at all but was designed to pump water out of mines. When you're a pioneer type, you make do, I guess.

Crash of the World's Largest (Ever) Aircraft: 1935

To this day, the world's largest aircraft was the Navy's USS *Macon*, based at Moffett Field near San Francisco. The helium-filled dirigible had a rigid aluminum frame and weighed 108 tons deadweight. With its helium bags filled, it could lift itself and 71 tons of freight and passengers. Alas, in 1935, the behemoth met rough winds off the Big Sur coast, where it crashed and sank into the ocean. Fortunately, all but two of the 83 crew members were able to escape. The sinking of the *Macon* became a symbol of the times, as the country itself suffered through the Great Depression.

All Ye Beer Drinkers, Bow Down

Richard Spikes, an African American man from San Francisco, developed and patented the beer keg tap in 1910. Talk about forward thinking! Spikes had more serious concerns on his mind, however. The ingenious inventor came up with many innovations, including automobile directional signals (a.k.a. your turn signals), automatic safety brakes, an improved gear system and transmission for cars and a drafting machine for blind people. On the more whimsical side, he developed and patented a horizontally swinging barber chair, an automatic car washer and a self-locking rack for billiard cues. Now where, I ask you, would we be without those items?

Gorilla Love

Primatologist Dian Fossey, who gained recognition for her work with mountain gorillas in Rwanda, grew up in the San Francisco Bay Area, graduating from San José State College (now San José State University) in 1954. After traveling to Africa and meeting renowned paleontologist Louis Leakey, Fossey established the Karisoke Research Center in Rwanda, where she studied the primates. In an attempt to publicize the need to preserve the gorilla's dwindling habitat, Fossey wrote *Gorillas in the Mist* (1983). Sadly, her fight to preserve the gorillas created antagonism among some of the local Africans and may have lead to her murder in 1985. Her book was made into a movie with the same title in 1988.

A Nuclear Power Plant on a Fault Line!

The first nuclear reactor to be decommissioned in the U.S. and, we hope, the only one located on an earthquake fault line is PG&E's Humboldt Bay Nuclear Power plant. Standing four miles south of Eureka, the reactor operated from 1963 until 1976, when the utility shut it down for refueling. Fortunately (or unfortunately, if you were an investor), a geologist's study turned up major fault lines under or near the reactor. The cost of seismic retrofitting and the public outcry were both so great that the company never reopened the reactor. Decommissioning work began in 2006.

Was There Life Before Macs?

Computer nerds extraordinaire, Steven P. Jobs and Steve Wozniak tinkered with electronics in what is today called Silicon Valley and came up with a clunky prototype of the first Apple computer. The two buddies finished the first circuit board in 1976. It had no keyboard, case, sound or graphics. In fact, when it was finished, it looked a whole lot like a 1970s stereo receiver that someone's little brother had dissected for fun.

Meg Whitman CEO of eBay

Business powerhouse Meg Whitman, CEO of eBay, is credited with making the company the huge success it is today. With a résumé that included the global marketing of Mr. Potato Head, she was a shoo-in for the job. Whitman moved to San Francisco in 1988 to take the CEO position at a budding Internet company called AuctionWeb. With Whitman in charge, eBay doubled its profits in the first quarter to $85.8 million and has continued to grow briskly ever since. In 2005, *Forbes* magazine named Whitman as one of the five most powerful women in the U.S. Her estimated personal worth of $1.6 billion also makes Whitman one of the richest people on the planet, *Forbes* said.

Nobel Prizes in Science

The list of Northern Californians to receive the Nobel Prize in scientific fields is long, illustrious and, at times, a bit esoteric.

☛ Willard Libby grew up in Sebastopol and went on to take the 1960 prize in Chemistry for inventing carbon-14 dating, which determines the age of archaeological and geological samples.

☛ UC Berkeley researcher Yuan T. Lee took honors in Chemistry for his contribution to "reaction dynamics."

☛ Oakland native Thomas C. Schelling took the 2005 prize in Economics for "having enhanced our understanding of conflict and cooperation through game-theory analysis" (whatever the heck that means).

☛ UC San Francisco neurologist Stanley Prusiner won the 1997 award in Medicine for discovering the prion, the infection mechanism for bovine spongiform encephalopathy (also known as mad cow disease).

Linus Pauling

Linus Pauling (1901–94) was one of only four laureates in history to receive two Nobel Prizes, receiving the 1954 prize in Chemistry and the 1962 Peace Prize for his efforts to halt aboveground nuclear testing. Although he spent the majority of his career at SoCal's Cal Tech, Pauling wised up and moved to Northern California in his later years. Pauling was diagnosed with a fatal renal disease in 1941 at the age of 40. With the help of a Stanford physician, Pauling controlled the disease using diet and vitamins. This personal success with alternative medicine may have been what launched him on the research (some called it obsessive quackery) of his later years, studying the health effects of high doses of vitamin C. Pauling founded the Institute of Orthomolecular Medicine, later renamed the Linus Pauling Institute of Science and Medicine, in Menlo Park in 1973. He lived to be 93, not bad for a man with a fatal illness.

COMMON CRIMES

How Dangerous is the Golden State?

California's crime rate, including rape, burglary and homicide, sits firmly at the national average, according to the FBI. With Washington, D.C., at a scary rate of 8836 in 1998 and sleepy New Hampshire at the nation's lowest rate of 2420, California's rate came in at 4343 for that year and is declining.

Yikes

The homicide rate in California has increased significantly since 2000—from 5.9 deaths per 100,000 people to 6.8.

If you're female, you're pretty safe—your death-by-homicide rate hovers around 2.3 per 100,000 in the state.

The most commonly used weapon in murders is a gun. No big surprise there. What did you expect—a candlestick? The most common reason given for murder is an argument (43 percent of the time) or gang-related activities (34 percent of the time).

Is the Foe a Friend?

The majority of killers, at least in sunny California, are acquainted with their victims—62 percent to be exact—of which about one-third not only know the unfortunate soul but are actually a family member. As the old saying goes, with friends and family like that…

And the Victims Are…

Although countless Hollywood films try to convince you otherwise, the vast majority of murder victims in California are not scantily clad, voluptuous young women, but are actually men. Eight-two percent of those killed are male. Most of those are young—57 percent are between 18 and 34 years old—and of either Hispanic (44 percent) or black (30 percent) heritage.

Rape

This category has an interesting title in the crime stats, "forcible rape." Causes one to wonder, "forcible rape" as opposed to what—consensual rape? In any case, fortunately the numbers of rape cases in California have decreased in the last 10 years, from 10,550 cases in 1995 to 9598 in 2004.

Domestic Violence

The numbers of domestic violence calls for assistance has decreased in the last 10 years, down by 19 percent since 1993 to about 194,000 in 2003. Fortunately, the proportion of these calls involving a weapon are down even more and is now sitting at 38 percent.

Strange to Say

Prior to 1986, domestic violence was not considered criminal conduct under California state law. Before that, it was what—just the everyday tussling between loved ones?

Burglary—Hip, Hip, Hurray!

In terms of burglary, especially, California law enforcement officials deserve kudos. (Either that or the population has simply grown less likely to covet their neighbors' assets.) In the last 20 years, the burglary rate in the state has declined steadily from a high of 1836 crimes per 100,000 people in 1983 to a 2005 rate of 674.

LOCAL LAWS OF INTEREST

Here, Birdie
Berkeley might be a relaxed place where hippies still linger, but don't be caught whistling for your canary before 7:00 AM. You may be cited.

Excuse Me
There's nothing more annoying than all those tourists and children licking away at their ice cream and blocking the sidewalk! There ought to be a law. Well, I'm kidding (mostly), but in Carmel, some Grinch-like individuals passed an ordinance banning the eating of ice cream while standing on the sidewalk.

The Crystal Ball
Don't tell folks in Santa Clara County to have a nice day or that you're sure everything will work out for them. It's illegal to tell someone's fortune in that county, even for free.

Let Parading Horses Parade

If a horse walks past you in a parade in Alameda County, be sure you don't bother it. That's against the law. The obvious trouble here is, how do you know what bothers any given horse? I mean, what if the sight of pink pants happens to send Mr. Ed into conniptions? How could I possibly know that, officer?

What Color is Your News Rack?
If it's anything other than red in Alameda County, you're busted.

Got a Tiger in your Tank?
Not in San Mateo County, you don't. Not without a permit. You are required to have a special permit in that county for tiger ownership.

Would You Like Water With That?

In Santa Clara County, it is illegal for a waiter in a restaurant to give a customer water unless he or she has specifically asked for it.

The End of Hog Heaven

All good things must come to an end, they say. On January 24, 1847, pigs were no longer allowed to run free in San Francisco (until the 1960s, but that's a different topic entirely). Yes, it was a sad day when the city decreed: "All stray hogs…must be securely penned or the hogs will be confiscated." For those whose piggies ran loose? A stiff $5 fine.

Word Has It

A number of oddball laws are on the books in other parts of California. Here are some examples:

☞ It's against the law for animals to attempt to…er, procreate within a 1500-foot radius of the nearest bar, school or church. There are several obvious problems here, not the least of which is who will pay for all those measuring tapes for the town dogs and cats.

☞ It's illegal for a man to buy liquor without written consent from his better half. (That one goes without saying, I think.)

MOST DANGEROUS PLACES

Scary Streets?

What is Northern California's most dangerous city? It's Oakland, according to the private research group Morgan Quitno, publishers of *America's Safest (and Most Dangerous) Cities*. This East Bay city, just across the water from San Francisco, ranks number 21 nationwide but, in sleepy Northern Cal, it's the riskiest.

Okay, This Is Weird

While Oakland is the city with the highest crime rate in Northern California, Stockton-Lodi also looms large in terms of dangerous, crime-ridden metropolitan areas. Why, you ask, would agricultural Stockton in the heart of the San Joaquin Valley, have so much crime? I have no freaking idea. After all, the city boasts an annual Asparagus Festival, the historic Bob Hope Theater and the former name of Mudville. What more could people want?

Safest City

In terms of low crime rates, Sunnyvale, in the heart of Silicon Valley, is the comfiest place in northern California. In fact, it's rated among the top 10 safest cities in the entire nation. Fremont comes in number two in the state and ranks 25th nationwide.

Another city in the computer belt, San José, takes top honors in the country for the safest city with a population over 500,000. San Francisco follows close behind in the number eight spot.

If You're on Foot...

Watch out if you're on foot in Solano County. This mostly rural area about 45 miles northeast of San Francisco bears the dubious honor of being the most dangerous spot for pedestrians in the state with a "Pedestrian Danger Index" (some bureaucrats have nothing better to do than make up officious sounding titles for stuff) of 100. That's worse than L.A.

The safest places to stroll? The "PDI" points to Humboldt, Monterey and San Luis Obispo Counties.

NOTABLE CRIMINALS

Black Bart, the Stagecoach Robber

Known as "the poetic robber," Charles E. Bolton (a.k.a. Black Bart) lived an apparently respectable life in San Francisco. He was well read, polite and a snappy dresser—in short, a gentleman. The only catch was that occasionally Bolton liked to take the evening boat to Stockton and head into the hills for a little holiday. According to James E. Rice, a Wells Fargo & Company agent at the time, "Being a wonderful pedestrian, he [Bolton] would usually walk 40 miles into the mountains by nighttime. The next day he would rob a stage, and the only evidence he would leave would be a 'poem' in which there was some humor and occasionally a vulgar line." The stagecoaches were bringing money in and out of Wells Fargo Bank.

Bolton lived this way from 1875 until 1883, before the now-famous Sheriff Tom Cunningham of San Joaquin County captured the outlaw. Even the capture was gentlemanly. The story goes that Sheriff Cunningham searched the scene of one hold up and found a handkerchief. The famous robber was tracked down by finding the establishment where Bolton had his hankies laundered. No messy gunfights for this fellow!

Black Bart pleaded guilty and served just over four years in San Quentin Prison for his crimes. After his release, he disappeared and was never heard from again.

In California law enforcement circles, a "wobbler" is the term for a crime that can be charged as either a felony or a misdemeanor.

The Hounds

After the Mexican-American War ended, ex-soldiers of Colonel Stevenson's California Volunteers found themselves with too much time on their hands. The men lived in a tent they called "Tammany Hall" on Montgomery Street in the wild and woolly Gold Rush days of San Francisco. On July 1849, the Hounds used their military skills and youthful energy to attack a group of Chileans also camped in the city. Having no police department, 230 volunteers were deputized to form the "Law and Order Party" in response to the attack. The new deputies arrested many of the Hounds. A Grand Jury indicted the men, and 24 Hounds were convicted of conspiracy, riot, robbery and assault with intent to kill. Justice moved rapidly in those days—all of this took place in the span of one week.

Boss Ruef

Intelligent and creative San Francisco lawyer Abraham Ruef got a bit too creative with the law in early 20th-century San Francisco. Ruef was hired by public utility companies to represent their interests. He saw no reason to spare expense in pursuit of this goal. When Ruef represented United Railroads of San Francisco in their effort to convert cable cars to electric trolleys, for instance, the lawyer split $85,000 (of his $200,000 attorney's fee) among the members of the city board of supervisors. Nice man. And, well, what do you know? The supervisors supported the railroads' ordinance just as Ruef had hoped. Ruef engaged in similarly corrupt deals on behalf of the water, gas, electric and telephone companies.

San Francisco citizens rose up in protest. They succeeded, after widely publicized trials, in removing the corrupt city officials from office and throwing Ruef in prison. The utility company executives, however, avoided punishment.

The Sampson Twins of Petaluma

Twin brothers Tony and Lloyd Sampson kept law enforcement officials on their toes in the rural town of Petaluma throughout the 1970s and '80s. The twins seemed to want to make the town a better place, but they picked unorthodox ways to show their civic concern, such as taunting a meter maid to protest parking fees. The incident led to a meter-maid-cart chase through the town, with eventual police involvement. The twins also attempted a civilian arrest of a judge. After a failed run for mayor (both of them as a double-header), the Sampsons finally cooled their heels in prison for setting off a firebomb in the car of the woman who beat them in the mayoral race. Talk about sore losers!

Preparedness Day Bombing, San Francisco: 1916

As the nation prepared to mobilize for World War I, San Francisco held a Preparedness Day Parade in 1916. When a bomb blast interrupted the festivities, killing 10 people and wounding 40 others, it didn't take city officials long to round up known radical Labor leader Thomas Mooney and his assistant, Warren Billings. The bombing was a terrible event, and the "justice" afterwards was equally unfortunate. Never mind that the evidence was full of perjury and false testimony, the two men were thrown in prison with life sentences. By 1939, the lack of evidence was so apparent that Governor Culbert Olson pardoned the men and they were released, after spending 20 years in prison for nothing. The true bomber was never found.

Governor "Sunny Jim" Rolph: 1930s

His demeanor was cheerful enough to earn him the nickname "Sunny Jim," but this governor of California must have been sick the day his civics class covered due process. When two men were arrested for kidnapping and murdering a prominent San José citizen, Governor Rolph said that he would not intervene if a mob decided to punish the prisoners. Emboldened, an angry crowd of vigilantes broke down the doors of the Santa Clara County jail and lynched the accused men in the street. Rolph promised a pardon to those involved, should they be arrested, and even said that he'd like to release all accused kidnappers to "those fine, patriotic San José citizens who know how to handle such a situation."

The "Twinkie Defense"

In San Francisco, on November 27, 1978, Dan White, a former city supervisor, climbed in a city hall window. Inside the building, he shot and killed two city officials, Mayor George Moscone and Supervisor Harvey Milk, the nation's first openly gay elected official. White's lawyer got him off on a "diminished capacity" defense. Because it came up in the trial that White had taken to eating Twinkies and a doctor testified that sugar might have exacerbated an imbalance in the accused's brain, the judgment became known as the "Twinkie defense." The public concluded that White had been let off because jurors believed that a Twinkie-induced malaise left him incapable of thinking clearly. In truth, the defense used White's Twinkie-eating as a sign that the otherwise health-conscious White was clinically depressed. White got off easy in court but later took his own life.

NOTABLE SPORTS FIGURES AND RECORD-BREAKERS

The "Say Hey Kid"

There are few names more famous in baseball than that of San Francisco Giants' centerfielder Willie Mays. Well loved for his enthusiastic attitude, Mays was more than just a nice guy; he racked up staggering career statistics, including 3283 hits and 660 home runs.

In 1951, Mays earned national Rookie of the Year honors with the New York Giants. In 1958, San Francisco became his primary team. He earned 12 Gold Gloves and played in four World Series and 24 All-Star games. Mays was inducted into the Baseball Hall of Fame in 1979.

Martinez-born Joe DiMaggio had a 61-game hitting streak in 1933 (eight years before his famous 56-game streak) while playing with the San Francisco Seals of the Pacific Coast League.

Knocking It Home

His snarly attitude and rumored steroid use do nothing to endear him to the media, but there's no arguing with San Francisco Giants' slugger Barry Bonds' talent. Bonds is one of the best (and by the time this book comes out, maybe *the* best) batter in major-league history.

This graduate of Serra High School in San Mateo has blasted through just about every batting record there is (or should I say "was"?). Seven times an MVP, Bonds had knocked 734 runs home by the start of the 2007 season, the most ever for a leftie and the second most in major-league history, beaten only by Hank Aaron.

World

Jerry Rice, widely considered to be the best wide receiver ever, holds 28 NFL records, including 1549 regular-season receptions and 33 more at the Super Bowl. Although he also played for the Raiders and the Seahawks, Rice is best remembered for his glory days with the San Francisco 49ers.

A standout in college, Rice was nicknamed "World" because people said there was no ball in the world he couldn't catch. Bill Walsh scouted the young player in 1985 and, in one of the best decisions he ever made, drafted the future Hall-of-Famer for the 49ers.

Rice started his career with a bang, recording 49 catches for 927 yards in his rookie season. He went on to serve as part of the classic Montana-Rice passing combo and to play in four Super Bowls. In 2002, he became the first player ever to catch a touchdown pass in four Super Bowls. Today, Rice lives with his wife and children in the San Francisco Bay Area.

Joe Montana

Considered the best post-season quarterback in NFL history, the 49ers' Joe Montana was golden in a clutch. Montana led the 49ers to victory at the Super Bowl no less than four times and earned MVP honors an amazing three out of those four. Taking the NFL passing title twice, Montana is considered second statistically only to Dan Marino.

Put Fear in 'Em, Baby

Longtime managing general partner of the Oakland Raiders Al Davis earned a reputation as a tough coach to beat and a tough person to deal with. His start with the Raiders in 1963 made him the youngest general manager/head coach in pro football. In just three seasons, Davis' 23–16–3 record got him named 1964 AFL coach of the year.

A better coach than a diplomat (a bit of an understatement there), Davis maintained a long feud with Commissioner Pete Rozell and, in 1980, began his contentious campaign to move the team to L.A. In spite of his wrangling, Davis' record was hard to beat. On his watch, the team won the AFL title in 1976 and Super Bowls in 1976, 1980 and 1983. When asked his secret, Davis reportedly said, "Our way is to put fear in the opponent, baby."

Madame Raider

The first female chief executive in the NFL, Amy Trask is with the Oakland Raiders. She reportedly lives for the game and even put off the start of her own wedding when a 1985 game went into overtime.

First Solo Pacific Crossing by Beer-Barrel Boat

The sought-after (well, maybe not so sought-after but definitely hard to win) title of "First Person to Make a Solo Voyage Across the Pacific Ocean by Beer-barrel Boat" goes to Kenichi Horie of Japan, who in 1999 headed out from San Francisco Bay and wound up in the Akashi Strait in Japan. His trusty 33-foot-long catamaran, *MALT's Mermaid II*, was made from used beer barrels.

Horie's choice of materials gained him sponsorship from Suntory, one of Japan's major breweries, but the sailor's goal was apparently the use of recycled materials in general. He used canvas made from recycled plastic bottles, for instance, for his junk-rigged sails.

Horie's first feat of sailing derring-do took place in 1962, when a 94-day trip ended in San Francisco, making him the first person to sail solo across the North Pacific. The 19-foot sailboat he used for the record-making crossing is on display in San Francisco's Maritime Museum.

DID YOU KNOW?

Legendary 49er Jerry Rice nearly danced his way to a win on the *Dancing with the Stars* reality TV show in 2006. He and his dance partner Anna Trebunskaya, considered the underdogs from the start, were beaten by only one team, singer Drew Lachey and his partner Cheryl Burke.

Special Athletes

Lindsay Mibach of Los Altos was named 2002 Special Olympian of the Year by the San José Sports Hall of Fame. Twenty-three-year-old Lindsay has been a Special Olympian for 15 years and earned the moniker "Cool Ice" as goalie for her floor hockey team.

Over 14,000 athletes with developmental disabilities, from eight years old and up, compete each year in the Northern California Special Olympics, hoping to win their way to the national event. The Special Olympics were started nationwide in the 1960s by Eunice Kennedy Shriver (a familiar surname to Californians today).

The Skating (Future) Surgeon

One Stanford University pre-med took a little time out of her studies to figure skate. During her freshman year, Debi Thomas won the national and world championships in 1986. Two years later, she went on to claim bronze for the U.S. at the Calgary Olympics, becoming the first African American woman to win a medal at the winter Olympics. She was inducted into the U.S. Figure Skating Hall of Fame in 2000.

MEMORABLE MOMENTS

The Catch, Number One

He ducked his head and ran flat out, according to one witness at the 1954 World Series, when San Francisco Giants fielder Willie Mays made a catch that has become baseball legend. Mays snagged Cleveland Indians Vic Wertz's fly ball over his shoulder and threw it in to rob Wertz of crucial extra bases. The catch—I mean, *the catch*—helped the Giants win that World Series in four games. This was the team's first series win since 1933 and, alas, their last so far.

The Catch, Number Two

San Francisco 49ers fans can give you every detail, but, basically, legendary Niners quarterback Joe Montana snapped the ball downfield to Dwight Clark in the 1981 NFC championship game to gain arguably the most important six yards in the team's history. The setting was Candlestick: third and three from the six-yard line with less than 90 seconds to go. A little pressure, boys? Clark's catch clinched the 49ers' Super Bowl bid (once they kicked the extra point) and was payback to the Cowboys, who had delivered a humiliating 59–14 defeat to the 49ers in the previous season.

DID YOU KNOW?

It was Al Davis who chose the Raiders' team colors of black and silver and helped design the famous pirate logo.

The "Immaculate Reception"

As far as Raiders fans are concerned there was nothing "immaculate" at all about the play that dashed the team's 1972 bid for the playoffs. There were only 22 seconds left in the AFC Divisional Playoff Game against the Pittsburg Steelers. With a 7–6 lead, the Raiders looked set to take the game, when Steelers quarterback Terry Bradshaw tossed a pass to running back John Fuqua. Fuqua fumbled the ball, under pressure from the Raiders John Tatum, but the Steelers Franco Harris recovered the ball and ran with it to the end zone. At first, it wasn't clear if it was a touchdown. (The ruling depended on which team had touched the ball last before Harris.) Referee Fred Swearingen made the decision that Pittsburg had scored. As most Raiders fans will tell you, the Steelers stole the game.

The Heidi Bowl

Okay, everyone who would rather watch *Heidi* than boring, old football raise your hands?

The Oakland Raiders–New York Jets game on November 17, 1968 featured 10 future Hall of Fame players in two of the Leagues' marquee teams. With 65 seconds to play, a Jets field goal gave them a 32–29 lead. The Raiders' kickoff took them to their 23-yard line. At that point, with fans on the edge of their easy chairs, the NBC network cut to a commercial break and came back with…*Heidi*.

Someone at NBC had decided to stick to the schedule, by gosh, and put *Heidi* on at 7:00 PM as planned. Millions of TV viewers didn't get to watch the rest of the game. (Can't you just see the beer and Cheetos flying?)

It was no ho-hum piece of football history to miss either. In a back-and-forth tussle, the Raiders scored two touchdowns in a nine-second span and then held on to a 43–32 lead. Needless to say, sports fans were not amused. Aw, come on, guys, Heidi's really cute.

World Series Earthquake

As the rivalry between the San Francisco Giants and the Oakland A's was unfolding in the 1989 World Series, an unexpected player stepped onto the field—Mother Nature. (Remember her from those margarine commercials?) After a 5–0 shutout victory for the A's in Oakland, Game 2 was about to start on October 17 in Candlestick Stadium. At exactly 5:00 PM, the pre-game formalities got underway with 30,000 fans in attendance. Four seconds later, the Loma Prieta Earthquake struck with all of its 6.9-on-the-Richter-scale force, knocking out power and causing the nearby Nimitz Freeway to collapse.

When the disaster was over and emergency crews had done their work, the quake had claimed 63 lives and injured thousands more, but the death toll was considerably lower than the 300 or so expected. Authorities attributed the spared lives to the fact that many people had left work early to watch the World Series, which was being broadcast on TV. Who says sports doesn't save lives?

By the way, after a respectful period, the A's went on to dominate the remainder of the series.

DID YOU KNOW?

Giants slugger Barry Bonds comes from an athletically talented family. His father, Dusty Baker, is a former Giants manager, while his aunt, Rosie Bonds, ran on the '64 U.S. Olympic team, when she held the national record for women's 80-meter hurdles.

Miracle On Ice

At the Squaw Valley Winter Olympics in 1960, the U.S. hockey team shocked the world by dumping the hugely favored Soviets 3–2. The Americans then went on to best Czechoslovakia 9–4 and take the nation's first gold medal ever in the event. Twenty years later, the team repeated its success at Lake Placid, NY.

POPULAR SPORTS IN THE STATE

Cold Water, Strong Currents and Huge Waves

When the average person hears about surfing, they might think Hawaii or Southern California, home of the Beach Boys–style surfer culture.

Elite surfers know that one of the gnarliest spots on Earth is a half-mile off the California coast near sleepy little Half Moon Bay. There the 20-foot monster waves known as mavericks, breaking over a boulder reef, have given the place its name—Mavericks.

Legendary surfer Jeff Clark, a native of the area, discovered the spot in 1968, though it took a while for the surfing world to believe that any place in California produced 20-foot waves. The phenomenon is real enough and, by now, well documented, with one giant swell on November 21, 2001, hitting the 100-foot mark, roughly the height of a 10-story building.

These days, elite surfers come from all over the world to compete in the Mavericks Surf Contest, started by Clark. *Sports Illustrated* called it the "Super Bowl of big-wave surfing."

Climbing the Nose

Yosemite's imposing El Capitan, a sheer 3000-foot-tall granite face, is the largest monolith in America. It's known as the place where modern big-wall climbing was invented.

Warren Harding was the first technical climber to succeed in scaling the Captain, beginning the ascent on November 1, 1958, with three teammates. On the evening of November 11, three of the four original teammates (one had withdrawn along the way) reached a ledge just below the summit. Harding couldn't resist. Working through the night, he drilled and bolted his way up the overhang, reaching the summit at about six on the morning of November 12, 1958.

All that work, and these days, proficient climbers can make the ascent in one long day. How things change.

Fast and Dirty

Mountain biking was one of those grassroots groundswells that resulted from a lot of warped, outdoor-loving adventurers (think four-year-olds on speed) who thought it would be fun to go bombing down (formerly) bucolic hillside paths on their bikes. It was grassroots because the idea seemed to occur to people in a bunch of different places at different times. Who would have ever guessed that the impulse would lead to a multimillion-dollar national fad?

Most mountain bikers agree, however, that the first real pioneers of the modern sport were northern Californians. The "Morrow Dirt Club" was a bunch of rag-tag bikers from Cupertino area who showed up at the West Coast Cyclocross Championships in Mill Valley in 1974 riding fat-tired bicycles with the first known derailleurs on them. (Invention of the first derailleur is attributed to Club member Russ Mahon.) Fellow mountain-bike pioneers Charlie Kelly, Joe Breeze and Gary Fisher from Marin County, who were also at the event, took notice. The Marin group took the idea and ran with it.

Strong Arm Tactics

Guys arm wrestling in Gilardi's Saloon in Petaluma, back in 1952, tested their strength against each other for fun. A young journalist in town decided to organize a real competition. He teamed up with other locals to form first the Petaluma, then the Northern California, then the California, and finally the World's Wristwrestling Championships. And, yes, they're still held in Petaluma.

The rest of the world was introduced to the championship mainly through coverage on *ABC's Wide World of Sports*, which started broadcasting the annual muscle-off in 1969.

One local Petaluma boy has made good at the championships year after year. Heavyweight Eric Woelfel won or placed in numerous championships, for both left- and right-handed competition. If the name sounds vaguely familiar, that's because he's my brother. (Aw, isn't that cute, the proud sister?)

The Squaw Valley Winter Olympics

In 1960, Northern California hosted the Winter Olympics by the shores of Lake Tahoe. At the time, Squaw Valley, the hosting ski area, had all of four double chairlifts and a rope tow. Stylin'! (Today, the resort offers 32 lifts, including an aerial cable car and a super gondola.) Here are a few of the highlights of those games:

☞ It was the largest Winter Games to date, with 34 nations competing.

☞ The U.S. Men's Hockey team took its first gold, as mentioned above ("Miracle on Ice").

☞ It was the Olympic debut for men's biathlon (you know, ski and shoot) and women's speed skiing.

☞ Walt Disney himself orchestrated the opening and closing ceremonies.

☞ It was the first Olympics to use "electronic" computers for result tallying.

☞ Tickets cost $7.50 per day and allowed spectators to see five major events.

☞ Lodging cost between $5 and $10 a night. (Those were the days!)

☞ Rain had washed out Squaw Valley's base, but just before the games began, storms dumped a fresh 12 feet of the white stuff.

☞ Those bloodthirsty athletes ate over 10 tons of meat during the games.

Famous Slopes

The Lake Tahoe area is home to some of the finest snow-sport areas in the world, including the famed resorts at Kirkwood, Heavenly Valley, Squaw Valley, Northstar, Sugar Bowl and Alpine Meadows. Visitors come for a range of sports such as snowmobiling, snowshoeing, cross-country skiing, telemark (or "tele") skiing, sledding and, of course, downhill skiing and snowboarding.

DID YOU  KNOW?

The 1960 Winter Olympics at Squaw Valley, Lake Tahoe, were the first Winter Games ever to be nationally televised.

Pedal to the Metal

The only NASCAR (that's car racing, for the auto illiterate) race that's run on a road course west of the Mississippi each year is at the Infineon Raceway, near the town of Sonoma. Formerly and still commonly known as the Sears Point Raceway, the track hosts nationally televised events including the NASCAR Nextel Cup and the IRL IndyCar Series.

If the revving of engines makes your blood boil, you can join the half-million car-racing fans who flock to Infineon each year. Thinking about getting behind the wheel yourself? Since it's a loop track, you'd better be really good at screaming around corners—to the left.

A couple of NASCAR records at the Sonoma raceway:

☛ Qualifying record holder: Jeff Gordon clocked in at 94.325 miles per hour on June 24, 2005.

☛ Fastest race winner: Ricky Rudd came in with a sizzling overall speed of 81.007 miles per hour at the June 23, 2002, event.

DID YOU KNOW?

Quarterback Joe Montana was passed over for the first two rounds of the 1979 NFL draft before being picked up by the 49ers.

Sports in a Theater?

One San Francisco acting troupe has earned a reputation for groundbreaking improvisational theater—and for being just a lot of fun. Bay Area Theatresports (BATS) started in 1986 and has been doing what theater critics call "bounce-in-your-seat funny" performances ever since.

The idea came from London Royal Court Theatre's Keith Johnstone. Johnstone sought a way to make theater as much fun as, and draw as big crowds as, spectator sports such as football. While working in England and then in Alberta, Canada, he developed a series of games in which actors develop their chops as they engage the audience in a competitive "act off" of sorts. The results are sold-out houses of hooting and hollering improv fans.

You can catch BATS (no net necessary) year-round at the 200-seat Bayfront Theater in San Francisco's Fort Mason Center.

Watch Out for Shark Bites

It's not just surfers who have to watch out for sharks these days. San José may not have any frozen lakes to speak of, but its hockey team is up and coming in a big way. Started in 1991 (after Oakland's California Golden Seals swam off to Cleveland), the San José Sharks have been building power and skill to become National Hockey League contenders.

FIRSTS OF ALL KINDS

Firsts

Northern California is reputed to be the place where the martini was invented, as well as the Frisbee, the Jacuzzi, the computer mouse, boysenberries, blue jeans and the beer-keg tap, to name just a few items dreamed up by the region's innovators.

Spanning the Distance

The Golden Gate Bridge spans the Golden Gate Strait that divides San Francisco from Marin County. A marvel of modern architecture, it was the longest suspension bridge in the world when it was built. The lesser-known Verrazano Narrows Bridge in New York City took the title away in 1964.

Here are a few interesting facts about the Golden Gate Bridge:

☛ Work began on the bridge on January 5, 1933.

☛ It officially opened on May 27, 1937.

☛ It cost $35 million to build.

232

☛ Eleven men died during its construction.

☛ It took more than 25 million worker hours to complete.

☛ The bridge measures 6450 feet long and weighs 22,000 tons.

☛ The longest single span measures 4200 feet.

☛ There are 80,000 miles of cable used throughout the bridge.

☛ In 1938, 3.5 million vehicles traveled the bridge.

☛ Just 40 years later, in 1978, 36,569,754 vehicles made the journey across.

The First Popsicle

Quite by accident, 11-year-old Frank Epperson created the first Popsicle. The story goes that in 1905, the San Francisco youngster made himself a drink mixing a flavored powder with soda water and then apparently left it, stick and all, on his front porch. Freezing nighttime temperatures meant Frank woke to a frozen treat, which he shared with his friends, who couldn't get enough of it. So rather than a lemonade stand, Frank started selling these icy concoctions. But it wasn't until 1923 that the then-29-year-old Frank acquired a patent. The name Popsicle was apparently Frank's children's contribution, crediting their pop with the creation of their icicle treat, hence "Popsicle."

DID YOU KNOW?

Originally under Spanish rule, San Francisco was first named Yerba Buena.

A Flurry of Firsts

☛ The world's largest underwater sand dunes can be found just off the coast of San Francisco, thanks to frequent tidal currents in the area. According to the U.S. Geological Survey, these dunes measure 700 feet in length and as much as 30 feet in height.

☛ At roughly 10 miles in diameter, a circle of mountains called the Sutter Buttes near Yuba City is thought to be the "world's smallest mountain range."

☛ Jackson is home to one of the world's deepest gold mines. The Kennedy Gold Mine got its start back in 1860 and kept producing until 1942. What remains today is an historic tourist attraction with 50 miles of excavations going as deep as 5912 feet into the earth's soil.

☛ The Mendocino National Forest has a unique claim to fame. Back on November 12, 1981, the first helium-filled balloon to cross the Pacific Ocean landed there after an 84-hour-and-31-minute journey from Nagashimi, Japan.

☛ One of the world's largest landlocked harbors is San Francisco Bay. It measures 60 miles in length and 3.5 miles in width.

☛ The San José Flea Market started out with 20 vendors and about 100 customers in 1960, but today it's considered to be America's largest open-air market.

☛ Folks in San Francisco must be mighty proud of their ballet company. The San Francisco Ballet is the oldest ballet company in the country and was the first to produce *Swan Lake* (1940) and *The Nutcracker* (1944).

☛ This has got to be some kind of record. Back in 1909, operators working out of San Francisco's Chinese American Telephone Exchange were expected to be multilingual. Aside from English, they had to be fluent in five Chinese dialects.

- Mono Lake is considered one of the oldest lakes in the Western Hemisphere.

- At a combined height of 2425 feet, the Upper and Lower Yosemite Falls, found in Yosemite National Park, are America's tallest waterfalls and the fifth tallest in the world.

- Home to little more than 3500 people, Weaverville has a record of its own. The town is home to Weaverville Drug Store, California's "oldest operating pharmacy." Established in 1851, the store has collected an assortment of antique pharmaceutical paraphernalia that it proudly displays for all to see.

- Gilroy calls itself the "Garlic Capital of the World" and celebrates with a garlic festival every year.

- Tehama County claims to hold the nation's largest three-day rodeo.

- The California State Railroad Museum, located in Sacramento, is the "largest museum of its kind in North America."

Forever in Blue Jeans

Blue jeans have been such a part of U.S. culture since the '60s that it's easy to forget that they've been around so dang long. San Francisco canvas salesman Levi Strauss noticed how tacky the gold miners looked back then in the 1850s and he thought to himself, "B'god and b'gosh, them fellas could use a fashion makeover." Strauss stitched together some canvas into the shape of pants and started selling them. The stiff things were reportedly not very comfortable (acid-washing came along later), but they held up to the rough-and-tumble prospector's life. Other working people, such as ranchers and cowboys, learned of the sturdy pants and started buying them, too. The dark blue color was intended to conceal stains.

Oldest Italian Restaurant in America

The Flor d'Italia, in San Francisco's famously Italian North Beach area, first opened in 1886 in order to serve the (other) appetites of patrons of the bordello across the street. The restaurant has been serving up pasta and such ever since.

The restaurant has come crashing down, quite literally, twice since it first opened. The building burned to the ground in 1893. Not so long afterwards, the new digs were destroyed by the 1906 earthquake. The "Flor" cooks weren't daunted by the tremor. They served the local population great kettles of soup out of a tent for a year while the restaurant was rebuilt. Today you can dine at the "Flor" at 2237 Mason Street. (You might want to wear a hardhat, just in case.)

Now That's a Big Rock

The town of Magnalia in Butte County claims the largest gold nugget ever found in America. The nugget unearthed there in 1859 weighed a hefty 54 pounds. (That's 787.5 troy ounces, for those of you in the know.) Out of that, 49.5 ounces were pure gold.

The First House in Oakland

A Massachusetts-born ship captain and would-be gold miner (who wasn't, in those days?), Moses Chase built the first house in Oakland at 404 East Eighth Street. He pitched his tent in the winter of 1849 at the foot of what is now Broadway and eventually was ready for a real roof over his head.

Doff Your Cap, Sir

Some customs are so familiar it never occurs to us to think that someone somewhere initiated them. Take, for instance, the custom of standing and removing your hat when the American national anthem is played. One Rossell O'Brien is credited with starting that tradition. O'Brien was a Civil War veteran who rose to the rank of brigadier general before retiring. Why did he make the gesture? Who knows? And why did the fad catch on? Again, no clue. We do know that the trendsetter is buried in Mountain View Cemetery.

First Wildlife Sanctuary

Before either Yellowstone or Yosemite National Parks were established, Oakland was home to the first wildlife preserve on the continent of North America. Many well-to-do residents of Oakland were fond of shooting their supper from the ducks on Merritt Lake. As the land around the lake developed, they declared the lake itself as a nature preserve.

Black Ahab

In the 1870s and '80s, William T. Shorey became the first African-American captain on the U.S. West Coast. Although born in Barbados, Shorey married and settled down in Oakland in 1887. With Shorey at the helm, his ship and her crew survived two typhoons and treacherous icepacks in the Bering Sea. His skill and daring earned him the nickname "Black Ahab," after Herman Melville's famed captain. He retired alive—a rare event for ship captains in those days—in 1908.

Oldest Lighthouse

Point Pinos Lighthouse, at the southern end of Monterey Bay, is California's oldest operational lighthouse. It's run these days by the Pacific Grove Museum of Natural History.

Flying Free

The man credited with inventing the modern Frisbee, Ed Headrick, did so while working at Wham-O in Emeryville in 1964. (He improved on a design already in existence.) He also invented Frisbee golf in the 1970s.

Headrick later retired to La Selva Beach, south of Santa Cruz, where he eventually died. When Headrick passed on in 2002, his family had his ashes incorporated into commemorative Frisbees. What else would you do with this guy? This was per Headrick's request, apparently because he had said that he'd always wanted to fly.

First in Frisbee

Working for the Wham-O company, Ed Headrick refined the Frisbee design that two friends, Warren Franscioni and Fred Morrison, had created in San Luis Obispo back in 1948. Franscioni and Morrison, like many people during the Depression, played catch with tin pie plates. But they decided to improve the flying disk's design by making it a little less noisy when it hit the ground and easier on the hands to catch. The two experimented with the new sensation of the day. As they said in the movie *The Graduate*, "Just one word—plastics!"

Fortune Cookies

So, you get fortune cookies at Chinese restaurants. That means they're Chinese, right? Not!

The first fortune cookie didn't wend its sweet, crunchy little way to China until 1992! Where were fortune cookies invented? That question is a little harder to answer. There are two claimants to the throne of fortune-cookie creator. One of them, David Jung, was from L.A. so, in this book's general mood of Northern California chauvinism, I'm going to say no more about him. The other inventor was Makoto Hagiwara of…(drumroll, please) San Francisco. Now, that's interesting.

Hagiwara was the landscape gardener who designed Golden Gate Park's famous Japanese Tea Garden. The story goes that an anti-Japanese mayor fired Hagiwara. When public outcry got the talented gardener re-hired, Hagiwara came up with a cookie to thank those who had spoken out for him. Each cookie contained a thank-you note. Hagiwara began serving the sweet bits of gratitude regularly at the Tea Garden. The 1915 Panama-Pacific Exhibition even displayed Hagiwara's cookies as part of the world's fair.

It Never Rains in California…

…unless you are in Del Norte Coast Redwoods State Park, that is. The park's name gives you a big hint that the place is located in the north where the weather gets a lot wetter. The park website advises: "Dress for rain." Located about one hour north of Fort Bragg, Del Norte gets the heaviest annual rainfall in the state: an average of 92 inches.

Cable Car Bell Ringing Contest

Back in 1949, a contest was held to choose the best cable car bell-ringer in all of San Francisco. Alexander Nielsen, of Cal Cable, took the honors that day. He was sent, along with two Muni gripmen, to the Chicago Railroad Fair, where they showed off Powell Car No. 524.

The cable car's trip to Chicago was poignant because San Francisco's mayor had nearly succeeded in shutting the cable cars down two years earlier and replacing them with buses.

In 1955, Mayor Elmer Robinson reinstated the Cable Car Bell-Ringing Contest as part of a festival to promote the cable cars. Ironically, even as he promoted them as a tourist attraction, Robinson was cutting back the cars' service. In spite of the mayor's mixed motives, the 1955 festival made the bell-ringing contest an annual event in the city's Union Square.

TEN (OR SO) GOOD REASONS TO LIVE IN NORTHERN CALIFORNIA

1. Need I Even Say It? Sunshine.

California is a great place to avoid SAD (seasonal affective disorder), that winter depression that comes from lack of light. The number of clear days per year in San Francisco, known locally as a foggy city, is 160. Hop over to Fresno and you enjoy a whopping 194 sunny days a year.

Compare that with 71 clear days in Seattle, 125 in Salt Lake City, a surprisingly low 90 clear days in Honolulu, and a heartbreaking 12 clear days a year in the town of Cold Bay, Alaska. You get the idea.

2. It's Not Southern California.

Ha, ha. Just kidding, dudes. It's important to keep the old north-south rivalry alive. Keeps life spicy.

3. What a Deal!

Students in California's community college and state university systems pay by far the lowest student fees of any institution in the country. University of California students pay the second lowest fees in the nation, though this is true for in-state students only. You can't pretend to be a Californian—we'll recognize you by your fear of hugs! (See number nine.) On the other hand, all you have to do is live here for a year to establish residency.

4. Earthquakes!

Gotta love 'em. Everybody needs to be reminded of the power of Mother Nature once in a while, don't they? People in Florida prefer hurricanes; those in Iowa like their dose in the form of twisters; residents of Saskatchewan prefer to get buried in snow. Here in Northern California, we like to shake it up from time to time.

5. The Sierra Nevadas.

While the Donner Party had, shall we say, a less than awesome time in them (see the Historical Happenings chapter for gory details), the Sierra Nevada mountains are an incomparable presence in California. Whether you like to ski, snowboard, backpack, mountain bike or just stare in awe, there's nothing like them. In Vermont, your balaclava freezes to your face after one run, while spring weather in California can be so sweet that skiers and boarders often wear shorts and t-shirts.

6. It's a Great Place to Be a Realtor.

That's the good news. Of course, if you'd like to buy a house, forget it. Not to put too fine a point on it, but the statewide median price for a home in 2006 was $576,000.

7. The Arts—A Wild Ride.

Whether you admire Frank Lloyd Wright's lean modern designs or Julia Morgan's warm Mediterranean-style, Diego Rivera's murals or Ansel Adams' photographs, Alice Walker's heartfelt novels or George Lucas' blockbuster films, whether you're a Deadhead or a follower of Michael Tilson Thomas' baton, Northern California's arts scene is, and always has been, unconventionally creative.

8. Diversity.

As of the year 2000, there is no majority ethnic group in California. And the future looks even more diverse, with schools counting 46 percent Hispanic or Latino, 33 percent white, 11 percent Asian, and 8 percent African American students. California promises to be a rich place indeed.

9. Hugs—Aw!

I couldn't find any numbers on this, but people really *do* hug you more here than any other place I've been—sometimes even people you have just met. I realize this has its pluses and minuses. Chalk it up to too many years spent out of state, but I'm not always up for getting pressed against some complete stranger's chest, myself. Like it or hate it, there is a certain warmth and innocence to the custom that is indicative of Northern California culture.

If you're coming out from New York City, you might as well just buy yourself a "Don't hug me—I'm from New York" t-shirt before you even set foot on the plane.

10. The Pacific Coast.

From Santa Barbara to Monterey, Santa Cruz to the Golden Gate, Point Reyes National Seashore to the little town of Arcata near the Oregon border, there can't be a more beautiful place on Earth than Northern California's Pacific coastline. I'm sure there must be at least a few as beautiful, but really none more. (Of course, I'm wildly biased.)

11. The Fruits—And I Don't Mean People.

With its extensive growing season, the San Joaquin Valley cranks out some of the tastiest produce you'll set lips to. Sample the sweet strawberries, kiwis, peaches, persimmons, figs…the list goes on and on. Travel a few hours north, and you're in the heart of California's wine country, where non-fruit delicacies include famous artichokes, almonds and olives.

12. Pride.

The San Francisco Bay Area, Northern California's main population center, often leads the nation, and even the world, in welcoming people of all stripes (sometimes literally). Love thy neighbor is a good thing in my book, even if she's a dyke on a bike who insists on revving her Harley before the parade starts. (See the Lifestyle chapter for details.)

13. Ah-nold.

I couldn't resist. But think about it—what other place gets to have the Terminator for its governor?

ABOUT THE AUTHORS

Monica Woelfel

Monica is a third-generation Californian. Family legend has it that her great-grandfather, a cobbler, made shoes for famed train robber Black Bart. As a member of the "Me Generation," Monica tried to break free of her hippie roots, but she now embraces brown rice, yoga, gardening and organic food—in other words, she's a perfect Northern Californian. She's written in almost every form you can imagine: nonfiction articles, creative nonfiction, screenplays, stage plays, fiction and poetry. Among her many jobs over her life, she's been an organic farmer, a cob house builder, an interpretive naturalist and a lab technician, as well as a reporter, editor and writer. Monica holds a bachelor's degree in biology from Swarthmore College and an MFA in creative writing from the University of British Columbia.

Lisa Wojna

Lisa Wojna, author of two other nonfiction books, has worked in the community newspaper industry as a writer and journalist and has traveled all over Canada, from the windy prairies of Manitoba to northern British Columbia, and even to the wilds of Africa. Although writing and photography have been a central part of her life for as long as she can remember, it's the people behind every story that are her motivation and give her the most fulfillment.

ABOUT THE ILLUSTRATORS

Patrick Hénaff

Born in France, Patrick Hénaff is now based in Edmonton. He is mostly self-taught and is a versatile artist who has explored a variety of media under many different influences. He now uses primarily pen and ink to draw and then processes the images on computer. He is particularly interested in the narrative power of pictures and tries to use them as a way to tell stories, whether he is working on comic pages, posters, illustrations, cartoons or concept art.

Roger Garcia

Roger Garcia immigrated to Canada from El Salvador at age seven. Because of the language barrier, he had to find a way to communicate with other kids, so he discovered the art of tracing. It wasn't long before he mastered this technique, and by age 14, he was drawing cartoons for the *Edmonton Examiner*. He taught himself to paint and sculpt; then in high school and college, Roger skipped class to hide in the art room and further explore his talent. Roger's work can be seen in a local newspaper and in places around Edmonton, Alberta.

Graham Johnson

Graham Johnson is an Edmonton-based illustrator and graphic designer. When he isn't drawing or designing, he...well...he's always drawing or designing! On the off-chance you catch him not doing one of those things, he's probably cooking, playing tennis or poring over other illustrations.

BLUE
BIKE
BOOKS

More madcap trivia from Blue Bike Books...

GROSS & DISGUSTING THINGS ABOUT THE HUMAN BODY

The human body may be a wonder of natural engineering, but it can also be pretty gross and bad-smelling. In this fearless little book, find the answers to such profound questions as why are boogers green, why do farts smell, and where does belly button lint come from? Dare to read on!

Softcover • 5.25" X 8.25" • 224 pages
ISBN-10: 1-897278-25-X
ISBN-13: 978-1-897278-25-3
$14.95

BATHROOM BOOK OF CAT TRIVIA

Read more about the most popular pet in North America in this great collection of feline facts. How long have felines existed in North America? How high can a cat jump? What do you call a group of cats? Find the answers to these questions and many more.

Softcover • 5.25" X 8.25" • 224 pages
ISBN-10: 1-897278-26-8
ISBN-13: 978-1-897278-26-0
$14.95

Available from your local bookseller
or by contacting the distributor,
Lone Pine Publishing
1-800-518-3541
www.lonepinepublishing.com